Programs for People in Crisis

A Guide for Educators, Administrators, and Clinical Trainers

Lee Ann Hoff &
Nina Miller

Foreword by
C. Everett Koop, MD, ScD

NORTHEASTERN UNIVERSITY CUSTOM BOOK PROGRAM

BOSTON

Designed by Ezra C. Holston
Illustrated by ScotGraphics

Northeastern University Custom Book Program

Library of Congress Cataloging-in-Publication Data
Hoff, Lee Ann.
    Programs for people in crisis.
    Bibliography: p.
    Includes index.
    1. Crisis intervention (Psychiatry) —Study and teaching.   2. Mental health planning.
    I. Miller, Nina.   II. Title.
    RC480.6.H65   1987   362.2'8   87–12317
    ISBN 0 – 89801– 012– 8 (alk. paper)

This book was composed in Fenice and ITC Berkeley Old Style by Monotype Composition, Baltimore, Maryland. It was printed and bound by Braun-Brumfield, Ann Arbor, Michigan. The paper is 60£ Natural Smooth, an acid-free sheet.

FOR

Frans Groot

George, Rachel, Kenneth, and Jennifer Miller

and

All the skilled and sensitive helpers who provide services for people in crisis

Contents

APPENDIX C: SAMPLE TRAINING AND EDUCATION MATERIALS

Foreword

For all human beings, life is the experience of pursuing basic needs: food, shelter, stable and loving relationships, meaningful work—a pursuit most possible in a climate of peace. But each year, millions of people are thrust outside this fundamental pursuit into the pain and chaos of crisis and thwarted in their need for safety, shelter, and social support. Instead of the joy of friendship, family, and community, some are victimized by the treachery of false friends, the violence of a wronged lover, the meanness of a parent, and the brutality of random vengeance. For others, the crisis may be intensely personal: an interior tragedy that attacks and devours its own host.

Good intentions—the outpourings of human charity—are needed for us to begin and to persevere; but such intentions, by themselves, are simply not enough. For the professional person in the fields of public health and social service, human charity is only the beginning of the process, not the end. And the process is not simple. If we are truly dedicated to bringing relief to a person in crisis, we must do our work in an organized, effective manner, one that promotes the physical, mental, and emotional healing processes. Therefore, we need to apply the knowledge and skills of all relevant disciplines to the human services we perform. There's nothing elementary about personal crisis, and there should be nothing elementary about our response to it either.

I especially favor having health and social services personnel look beyond the immediate crisis event and develop the means with which to prevent a repetition of the crisis. Preventive services, often delivered simultaneously with treatment, also require clarity of purpose and good organization to be effective over the long term.

The person in crisis, therefore, must receive service that is not only immediate and caring—but is also capable. And capability in service requires broad-gauge, systematic thought and action. Fortunately, over the past several decades, crisis leaders in our respective professions of public health, medicine, nursing, social service, law enforcement, and psychology have constructed a firm base of theory and practice upon which we can individually build strong and effective protocols for patient/client assessment, treatment, and follow-up. The emotional chaos that may immobilize a person in crisis must not be mimicked by the individual or the agency providing vital services to that person. Quite the opposite: we must make sure we meet—and overcome— the potential anarchy of personal crisis with the structure and rationality of appropriate organization and well-trained crisis managers.

That's what this book, *Programs for People in Crisis,* is all about, and I commend it to you.

June 1987

C. Everett Koop, MD, ScD
Surgeon General
U.S. Public Health Service

Preface

Purpose and Scope ██████████████████████████████

The AIDS epidemic continues unabated world-wide. Thousands of young people, especially in the United States, decide they prefer death over life and kill themselves in unprecedented numbers. Millions of people on all continents are victimized by violence, abuse, or the terrors of war or political conflict. Natural and man-made disasters continue to take thousands of lives and leave many homeless or stricken with the ill-effects of environmental hazards. The social and economic inequality of millions more leaves individuals, families, and entire communities doubly vulnerable to emotional crisis when tragedy strikes.

The challenge to human service workers to assist people in crisis is a daunting one. Necessary as it is to be there for distressed people, however, the risk of burnout and withdrawal also looms on the horizon if helpers are ill-prepared to respond according to professional and humanitarian ideals or are unsupported as they do so. The time for such preparation is not when people are face-to-face with crises, but rather, when we plan educational and service programs. In this book we stress the need for *anticipatory* preparation of professionals and others and comprehensive program planning to meet the growing need for crisis services in all health and human service fields.

Programs for People in Crisis addresses two urgent tasks in the crisis field: The international development and expansion of pre-service and in-service education programs for crisis practitioners in various human service disciplines: nursing, social work, psychology, general medical and psychiatric practice, educational, pastoral and rehabilitation counseling, victim assistance programs, and police work; and the expansion and refinement of programs to deliver high quality service to people in crisis.

The "chicken and egg" dilemma confronting educators, program administrators, and clinical trainers in crisis work hinders the successful accomplishment of these training and service tasks. It is also difficult, if not impossible, to establish service programs according to national standards without personnel specifically prepared in crisis theory and practice. Thus, the clinical training of crisis practitioners has often been sketchy, because supervised clinical practice settings have not been available to crisis trainees.

This source book is intended to assist educators, clinical trainers, and health and human service administrators in an effective *tandem* approach to this theory/practice dilemma. It presumes the inextricable relationship between excellence in clinical practice and educational and training programs. A major deficit in either of these facets of the crisis field produces a mutually negative effect, and will do disservice to people in crisis.

Programs for People in Crisis is not a clinical text. It is an *instructional* and *program development* guide that complements various clinical texts. However, we are not simply presenting an instructor's or supervisor's "cookbook" with all-purpose recipes. Rather, our intent is to provide broad *principles* for instruction and program planning, plus self-help sources and self-evaluation tools to serve as guidelines in this rapidly developing field. Our presentation of this framework for education/training and program development reveals our keen awareness of the need to tailor programs to the unique circumstances, resources, and constraints of individual institutions and their constituents: students, trainees, or people in crisis. We propose no monolithic model for either training or service programs, but rather, we emphasize national standards to guide the development and evaluation of specific programs.

Thus, we show how crisis training and practice can be integrated into existing human service programs. We also illustrate how formal crisis intervention complements rather than usurps what people have done intuitively for themselves and their loved ones for centuries.

Organization and Sources

Chapter 1 sets the tone by discussing background issues and current societal crises such as teen suicide, AIDS, victimization by crime, and disaster that underscore the urgent need for comprehensive crisis services world-wide. Chapters 2, 3, and 4 focus on educational and training programs. Chapters 5, 6, and 7 address program planning, organization, and management; Chapter 8 discusses the essentials of consultation and community education in crisis work. As a whole, the book stresses the importance of primary care and preventive intervention to avoid unnecessary human suffering and to address the central issue of cost containment in health service delivery. It thus contributes to achieving the World Health Organization goal of "health for all by the year 2000."

We avoid ivory tower theorizing and provide a practical resource for educators and human service personnel. In the topics addressed, we draw on our interdisciplinary preparation and experience in crisis intervention and related disciplines:

1. Higher education and curriculum development for health and mental health professionals (nursing, clinical and community psychology, social work, and rehabilitation counseling).
2. In-service training and consultation for hundreds of crisis and human service workers in various disciplines (nursing, social work, medicine, ministry, mental health counseling, police work, teaching, etc.).
3. Clinical practice, program development and administration of crisis programs in diverse urban and rural settings, and current work as Certification Examiners of the American Association of Suicidology, the national standard setting and accreditation body for comprehensive crisis services (crisis clinics, community mental health emergency programs, etc.).

Audience

We have addressed this book to an interdisciplinary audience since theory and practice in crisis work cross the boundaries of several disciplines. Specifically, we suggest the following uses and users of the book:

1. Educators and students in college and university programs preparing health, mental health, and other human service professionals—nursing, medicine, social work, clinical/community psychology, counseling, clinical pastoral training, etc. This audience might use the book as a companion volume to texts focusing on clinical skills in crisis intervention (see Appendix A).
2. Consultation, education, and training personnel in community mental health agencies, hospitals, victim assistance programs, police academies, EMT training programs, and related fields.
3. Students and instructors in university programs preparing human service administrators.
4. Administrators, program directors, and staff developers in health,

mental health, and other human service fields that offer (or receive requests for) crisis service on a full- or part-time basis. Staff of alternative human services such as shelters for battered women, rape crisis services, and substance abuse treatment centers will also find the book useful, especially since many of these programs rely heavily on non-professional personnel.

5. State and county mental health authorities, policy boards, and funding bodies for crisis services (e.g., United Way) will also profit from the book, particularly in its emphasis on national standards for the development of crisis service and training programs.

6. The general reader, especially consumers of crisis and mental health services who wish to evaluate the quality of care they receive in relation to recognized standards.

At this time in history more individuals and communities are conscious of their need for comfort and assistance during critical life events. Based on what increasing numbers perceive as their right, people are more vocal in demanding appropriate health care during crisis. We hope that this book will be a timely guide for educators, administrators, and clinical trainers in their efforts to provide what is expected by people in crisis and by those charged to help them.

Acknowledgments

While the final production of this book is very recent, the overall process of developing our approach to crisis education, service, and training programs grew from the wisdom and wealth of experience of many people we have come to know and respect over our years in the crisis field. The collaborative approach that we emphasize symbolizes the fruitful interaction we have enjoyed with many students, staff and board members, crisis trainees, and numerous others connected to the success of crisis programs. Without their openness to learning and their generous cooperation and feedback regarding specific program and training goals, the insights we share in this book would be much more limited. We thank every student, volunteer, colleague, and continuing education participant we have worked with in supervisory, teaching, and collegial relationships, as well as our own mentors who have shared their wisdom and support.

We also thank the reviewers of the manuscript for their constructive suggestions: Evelyn Barbee, RN, PhD, University of Michigan; Joan Grindley, RN, EdD, Northeastern University; Gwyn Harvey, MS, Life

Crisis Services, Inc., St. Louis; Karen McLaughlin, Massachusetts Office for Victim Assistance; and Myron Mohr, PhD, Baton Rouge Crisis Intervention Center, Inc.

At Northeastern University, we especially thank Ezra C. Holston, Director, Custom Book Program, for his dedicated work on publishing this book, and Sherry Anderson for her assistance in word processing and preparation of the index. Without their patience, good humor, support, and expertise, the resolution of various production problems would have been less than satisfactory. We also thank Dr. C. Everett Koop for writing the foreword, and Addison-Wesley Publishing Company for permission to reprint selected passages from *People in Crisis*.

Last but not least, we thank our families and friends for their support and patience through the usual ups and downs of producing a book. By their caring and concern, they remind us that taking care of each other is central to life and to success in crisis work.

June 1987   Lee Ann Hoff
                                                    Nina Miller

1

The Significance and Urgency of Crisis Services

The Crisis Model in Human Services ■■■■■■■■■■■■

DAVID JONES ■■■■■■■■■■■■■■■■■■■■■■■■■■■■■■

At 11:00 p.m. a police officer calls the 24-hour telephone crisis program. A team of professional crisis workers (a psychiatric nurse with a master's degree and a volunteer with a B.A. in psychology) makes an outreach visit to the home of David Jones, whom the police and Mr. Jones' family believe to be acutely suicidal, non-cooperative, and in need of assessment for possible involuntary hospitalization. Mr. Jones has refused police and family recommendations for treatment. The outreach team spends one-and-one-half hours with Mr. Jones and his family in their home. Mr. Jones finally agrees to go to the emergency department of a community hospital where he will be examined by psychiatric liaison staff for possible hospitalization. Following the assessment of Mr. Jones and his family situation, he remains overnight in the emergency department holding bed. Outpatient therapy begins the following morning for Mr. Jones and his family at the community mental health center where the hospital has an interagency service contract for follow-up of such mental health emergency cases. The family is given the telephone number of the 24-hour telephone and outreach crisis program where the police had originally called on behalf of this family (adapted from Wells and Hoff, 1984).

Many family members (natural crisis managers) and human service professionals (formal crisis managers) will be familiar with this crisis situation. The example highlights similarities between what family members and mental health professionals do in managing such a crisis, for example, listening and making judgments and decisions about what to do. In situations like this one and others, the work of the "natural" and "formal" crisis managers is complementary (Hoff, 1984a:24–29).

However, there are some differences. In this situation, one of the most obvious is that the crisis outreach workers and mental health professionals are attached to formally established programs offering crisis services. These workers possess knowledge and skills—acquired, presumably, through professional education or training—regarding crisis management that go beyond what "everybody knows" about people's needs in distress.

Crisis and crisis intervention, considered broadly, are as old as humankind. Helping people in crisis is intrinsic to the nurturing side of human character; humans possess the capacity to create a culture of caring and concern for people in distress. Thus, crisis intervention can be seen as a natural human action embedded in the culture and the process of learning how to survive through stressful life events among our fellow human beings.

In traditional societies, assistance and support to distressed people were available through the extended family and indigenous community leaders, a tribal chief or healer. In contemporary industrialized societies, social roles are more sharply defined, and individuals in trouble are more frequently left to their own devices when troubled. These social patterns have been accompanied by the growth of professionalism, emphasizing the training of various experts to deal with emotional and mental upsets. A major outgrowth of this trend is the development of the crisis model as a distinct body of knowledge and practice. During the past two decades, the popularity of this growing field of practice has been fueled not only by the service needs of people in crisis but also by cost containment issues. It is thus seen as an expedient and, at face value, less expensive form of "treatment," if for no other reason because of its brevity. These factors have led to an uneven development of the crisis field.

Complicating the uneven development of the field is the fact that few health and other human service professionals receive more than a few hours of content regarding crisis theory and practice during their formal preparation. This finding from a recent national survey (Berman, 1983) underscores the overlapping "natural" and "formal" crisis management roles. As members of the human community, we all know something about the management of life crises, so it is easy for health and social service professionals to avoid through rationalization the need for special training.

The language used by writers and practitioners contributes to some of the major issues and problems in the crisis field—crisis intervention, crisis therapy, crisis management, crisis counseling, emergency psychiatry, crisis work, crisis service, crisis program. Complementing this array of terms for services rendered are various descriptions of the people who render these services to people in crisis—crisis counselor, crisis therapist, crisis worker, crisis manager, professional, non-professional, and para-professional crisis workers. These interchangeable and sometimes confusing descriptions of the work and workers involved in the field reveal that crisis intervention is a very young area of human service practice. But these different descriptions also point to beliefs and assumptions about distressed people and what is to be done to assist them. As a basis for shared meaning and as an aid to the development of the field, the following definitions are used in this book (Hoff, 1984a; Wells and Hoff, 1984).

Crisis An acute, emotional upset arising from situational, developmental, or social sources and resulting in a temporary inability to cope through usual problem-solving devices.

Crisis management The entire process of working through a crisis to its endpoint of *crisis resolution*. It includes activities of the person in crisis as well as those of people helping the individual, e.g., a family member or formal crisis worker.

Crisis intervention That aspect of the crisis management process focusing on resolution of the immediate problem through the use of personal, social, environmental, and sometimes material resources. The process is carried out by a crisis worker—nurse, police officer, physician, psychotherapist, counselor, or minister. Crisis intervention is related to but differs from psychotherapy (see Hoff, 1984a: 4–9).

Emergency psychiatry A branch of medicine that deals with acute behavioral disturbances related to severe mental or emotional instability. It may overlap with crisis intervention but it also implies the need for distinct medical intervention such as medication or admission to an inpatient psychiatric service.

Crisis counseling An aspect of the crisis management process focusing particularly on the *emotional* ramifications of the crisis. A crisis worker with formal preparation in counseling techniques performs this process.

Crisis worker A person—paid or volunteer—who acquires specialized knowledge and skills in crisis work (including suicide and assault prevention), who adheres to the technical and ethical standards of the field, and who spends at least part of his or her time providing crisis intervention services. Crisis workers may include but are not limited to those possessing a professional mental health degree, e.g., psychiatric nurse, psychiatrist, psychiatric social worker, or clinical psychologist.

Crisis program A generic term describing the various organized agencies that provide services, e.g., emergency services of community mental health centers, suicide prevention centers, psychiatric or behavioral sections of emergency medical services, shelters for runaway teenagers, rape crisis centers, battered women's programs, and services for other victims of crime.

Client A term designating a person who uses the service provided by a crisis program. The client may be a brief "caller," a long-term mentally ill "patient" who becomes assaultive, a victim of crime, or a homeless, battered woman. In this book, "client" is sometimes used interchangeably with "consumer."

Every person working in health and human services—professional, paraprofessional, or lay volunteer—should understand the basic concepts and practices of the crisis model. Crisis intervention is not merely a "band-aid" version of psychotherapy. It is an organized approach to helping distressed people that can be mastered by lay people and professionals through a systematic educational/training program. While goodwill and peer support of volunteers (such as those working with AIDS victims, runaway teenagers and crime victims) are necessary, they usually are not sufficient. If people in these settings become suicidal or psychotic, further knowledge and expertise is necessary to assist them properly. Yet, to have credibility, mental health professionals who provide consultation to frontline workers need to have both training and experience in crisis outreach work. It is vital for various human service workers to combine their unique talents in a systematic and humane community program for diverse people in crisis (see case example David Jones). Thus, educators and trainers need to incorporate crisis concepts and practice strategies into programs preparing students and/or practitioners in human services.

Issues Affecting Crisis Services ▬▬▬▬▬▬▬▬

The urgency of developing or expanding crisis service and education/training programs is highlighted in the following case example.

JANE BARROW ▬▬▬▬▬▬▬▬▬▬▬▬▬▬▬▬▬▬▬

After an acute battering episode by her husband, Jane Barrow went by taxi to a local medical emergency facility for treatment of bruises and lacerations. While there, neither physician nor nurse inquired about her problems when she reported that her husband had beaten her. She then went to a local community mental health center on her own where she was given a prescription of tranquilizers and an appointment in one week. Jane went home feeling even more depressed than before she sought help.

This case illustrates that comprehensive crisis services (7-days-a-week, 24-hours-a-day in office and community settings) are far from routine in most communities, even though emergency mental health/

crisis service was declared an "essential element" of community mental health programs over 25 years ago by a Congressional Task Force.

The joint commission report

The report of this Task Force, *Action for Mental Health* (1961), laid the foundation for the community mental health movement in the United States. Through five years of study, it documented that people were not getting the help they needed, when they needed it, and where they needed it, close to their natural social setting. The report revealed that:

- people in crisis were tired of waiting lists,
- professionals were tired of lengthy and expensive therapy that often did not help because sometimes it came too late,
- large numbers of people (42%) went initially to a physician or to clergy for *any* problem,
- long years of training were not necessary to learn how to help distressed people,
- volunteers and community caretakers (e.g., police officers, teachers, and ministers) were a large untapped source for helping people in distress.

These findings are still relevant 25 years later. It is also noteworthy that the National Institute of Mental Health (NIMH) published the proceedings of its 1970 national conference to chart the course of suicide prevention and crisis intervention in the 1970s. This document is still relevant in the mid-1980s since the national agenda for suicide prevention and crisis intervention was displaced by issues of greater political popularity. One result is that most of the recommendations for the 1970s still need to be implemented. However, the federal government is addressing these critical issues as national attention focuses on adolescent suicide, AIDS (Acquired Immune Deficiency Syndrome), child sexual abuse, and the homeless, even as individuals and organizations such as the American Association of Suicidology continue their efforts in spite of limited public support.

National attention to victims

Recent government reports on victimization also point to the necessity of expanding crisis services and assuring that health, social service, and criminal justice workers receive basic training in assisting victims in crisis (President's Task Force, 1982; Attorney General's Task Force, 1984; Surgeon General's Workshop, 1986). These documents, along with crisis texts (e.g., Campbell and Humphreys, 1984; Hoff, 1984a; Burgess and Baldwin, 1981), reveal the importance of collaboration between various human service workers (health, social service, and criminal justice).

This issue is even more significant because of the life and death dimensions of many crisis situations. Here, the work of Morton Bard (1972) is instructive. The crisis intervention training programs for police officers developed by Bard in New York City resulted in a significant reduction in the number of injuries and deaths of officers on the job. Also, when officers made appropriate referrals of crisis cases to mental health facilities, most agencies had no crisis programs providing the immediate access to service demanded by these cases. (This situation is currently improving in some communities.)

The multi-faceted dimension of crisis intervention

A related issue in crisis work concerns the overlap between the emotional, social/political, physical, and material dimensions of particular crisis situations. For example, parents suffering the loss of an infant through SIDS (Sudden Infant Death Syndrome) need primarily emotional and social support. Unless prior psychopathology is present, peer support through a SIDS parents' group, and perhaps crisis counseling for the parents, often suffices. In contrast, if the crisis arises from personal injury through malice or neglect (such as rape or contamination by hazardous waste), some kind of social action (e.g., demanding victim compensation) is indicated in addition to the emotional support the person may need (Lifton and Olson, 1976; Gibbs, 1982; Hoff, 1984a). Overlapping roles are also relevant in helping people who are homeless through battering, fire, or flooding. Material aid must be combined with emotional and social support, plus social action if the origin of the crisis is social, as in the case of victimization by crime (Hoff, 1984b).

Another area for increased collaboration is between paraprofessional crisis workers and traditional psychiatric practitioners. Historically, paraprofessionals and lay people played a large role in responding to the urgent need for crisis programs. Their work grew out of the suicide prevention and alternative health care movement of the 1960s (Hoff, 1984a; Baldwin, 1975). Meanwhile, traditional psychiatric agencies were pressured to lend their professional expertise to the growing need for crisis services. Also, the 1965 call for a 24-hour crisis response through federal legislation for community mental health centers went unanswered for years in all but a few communities.

One result of these historical developments has been a false dichotomy between traditional psychiatric emergency care and crisis service arising from indigenous community sources. This dichotomy is visible in practice and coordination conflicts that have detrimental effects for people in crisis (see case example Jane Barrow). The dichotomy also highlights the need for more widespread knowledge about agency and individual practice standards, common concepts and principles guiding practice, and other interdisciplinary issues this book addresses. The Certification Committee of the American Association of Suicidology has addressed some of these issues in the past decade. This group stressed the importance of national standards for crisis service and training. Therefore in 1976, it launched a program to certify comprehensive crisis programs in the United States. The American Association of Suicidology, the national standard-setting body for crisis services, developed and directs this program. Certification assures consumers that the services provided by a certified crisis program meet at least the minimum standards in administration, training, and service delivery recommended by national crisis experts.

Research and theory development ■■■■■■■■■■■■■■■

Research and theory development is another issue in the crisis field. Even though historically important figures like Gerald Caplan (1964) and Erik Erikson (1963) emphasized cultural and social factors influencing the crisis experience, most United States-based sources reflect a psychodynamic emphasis and the dominant theme of individualism in American society (Bellah et al., 1985). Social and cultural sources of many crisis situations influence the current status of crisis theory development, particularly victimization by crime and the various forms of man-made disaster. In an attempt to fill the general sociocultural gap in crisis theory, Hoff developed from her research with battered women in crisis (1984b) a crisis paradigm (1984a, *esp.* Chapters 1, 2, 5, 8, 9, and 11) (see Figure 1.1). The social-psychological and cultural perspective of this paradigm, along with complementary works, exhibits the dominant theoretical underpinnings and values of this source book.

These issues underscore the multi-faceted and interdisciplinary aspects of the crisis field. The core elements of theory and practice

Figure 1.1

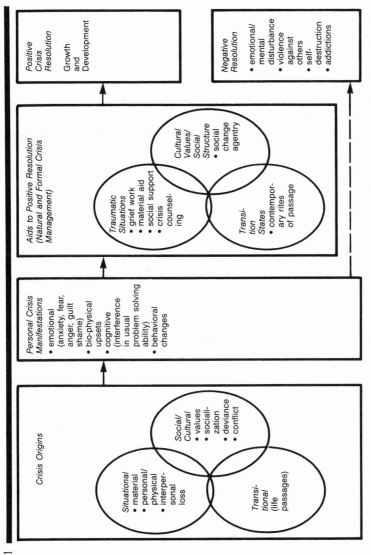

Crisis Paradigm. Crisis origins, manifestations, and outcomes, and the respective functions of crisis management have an interactional relationship. The intertwined circles represent the distinct yet interrelated "origins" of crisis and "aids to positive resolution," even though personal manifestations are often similar.

Originally printed in *People in Crisis*, 2nd ed. (Menlo Park., CA: Addison-Wesley, 1984); and *Violence against Women: A Social-Cultural Network Analysis*, PhD dissertation. (Boston: Boston University, 1984.) Reprinted with permission of publisher.

that apply to crisis workers must be identified, regardless of professional discipline and the settings in which crises occur (see Chapter 2). Thus, while crisis work is as old as humankind, the systematic approach to it by educators, practitioners, and administrators as an organized body of knowledge and practice is very new, only a few decades old. Therefore, we urge educators and practitioners to examine critically the concepts they choose for training and guiding service delivery (see Appendix A, Crisis Texts). The practice implications of theory selection are illustrated in Figure 1.2, depicting the relationship between educational or service philosophy, objectives, content, methods (of training or service delivery), and evaluation. The broad parameters of a comprehensive approach might include information based on a particular philosophy about the crisis experience, the people experiencing it, and the human service delivery system. In the last section of this chapter, we discuss examples that illustrate the influence of values, beliefs, and the theoretical underpinnings on educational/training programs, on program development, and on clinical practice.

Crisis Service Delivery: Differential Approaches

We have already stated that psychiatric or indigenous community groups deliver crisis service. Now, we elaborate on the different approaches that can be used in crisis work while preserving the core aspects of the crisis model that distinguish it from other forms of service, regardless of the person delivering it. This discussion lays the foundation for later presentation of CORE content and its application to different groups and in various settings (see Chapter 2).

Regardless of different approaches to crisis service delivery, four essential steps characterize the crisis management process:

1. Psychosocial assessment of the individual, family, or community in crisis. This always includes evaluation of the risk of suicide or assault on others.
2. Development of a plan with the person, family, or groups in crisis, based on assessment data.
3. Implementing the plan by drawing on personal, social, and material resources.

Figure 1.2

Philosophy/Values, Beliefs

Every citizen has a right to a service that is accessible and always available when in crisis.

Objectives

To provide a 24-hour response mechanism in office and community/home settings to citizens of X, Y, Z community (estimate units of service in relation to needs of population served.)

Content

24-hour telephone service, walk-in/office service, outreach service, and residential (holding beds for acute care).

Methods

24-hour staffing, comprehensive training of staff, consultation and back-up, and community networking.

Evaluation

Based on objectives, e.g., 500 units of service were projected; 485 were delivered.

Flow Chart Illustrating How Program Elements Flow from Philosophy.

4. Follow-up and evaluation of the crisis management process and resolution of the individual, family, or community crisis.

Individuals or family members in natural settings, or trained crisis workers in telephone, office, college residence hall, nursing home, social agency, community, hospital, or other settings can implement these steps. The essential steps of crisis management can also be carried out in specialized settings for crisis service, or they can be integrated with psychotherapy or other forms of human interaction. In natural situations, parents who know the warning signs of suicide can use these steps on behalf of their own child during the normal process of parent-child interaction. In formal settings, lay volunteers, mental health professionals, nurses, police officers, clergy, or others trained in crisis theory and practice can implement the steps of crisis management as a specialized service or with other kinds of needed service, for example:

- medical treatment of an accident victim (paramedics, nurses, and physicians),
- death notification or rescue of a rape victim (police),
- comfort of suicide survivors* (pastors, nurses),
- long-term treatment of emotionally and mentally disturbed people (technicians and other mental health workers),
- social service to abusive parents (social workers),
- support of battered women and other victims (various victim advocates),
- support of AIDS victims and their families, including friends or lovers (everyone).

Crisis work in some of these settings may be less than comprehensive because many health and human service workers lack training in the essential principles of crisis theory and practice. Crisis management training increases the probability of appropriate responses to the needs of people in stressful situations. Without such training, workers, like mental health professionals, may assume that expertise in psychotherapy suffices for crisis work, and lay volunteers may rely too much on goodwill and intuition. Inadequate training also perpetuates the notion that crisis management is just a variation of psychotherapy.

---

* "Suicide survivors" in this book refers to those people left (family, friends) after a person commits suicide. The term is sometimes used mistakenly to mean those surviving a suicide attempt.

While crisis intervention uses some common techniques in psychotherapy (e.g., active listening), it is important for health workers to distinguish between elements of the crisis model and other helping processes. (For further discussion of these distinctions see Hoff, 1984a: 17–21.) Being clear about the crisis model aids in its successful integration with various treatment programs for persons physically ill or emotionally/mentally disturbed, people who are generally more vulnerable to crisis than others.

The creative application of these basic elements of the crisis model will vary according to personal style and will be influenced by factors such as professional training in particular disciplines. Regardless of these individual variations, crisis trainers and practitioners should recognize the influence of their values and historical sources on their teaching and practice with people in crisis. Also, everybody involved in the crisis field needs to acknowledge the crisis approach's limits and the cultural meaning of the current popularity of the crisis model. While there is no substitute for 24-hour local response to people in acute distress, the crisis model needs revitalization as one aspect of "primary prevention," originally proposed by Caplan (1964), without neglecting its importance in secondary and tertiary prevention (see pp. 108–110). Crisis management must not be regarded as a panacea for all social, emotional, and mental problems.

The limitations of crisis intervention and the need to see it in larger sociocultural and political perspective are dramatically illustrated in the following vignette. McKinlay (1979:9) discusses the "manufacture of illness" and the futility of tinkering with "downstream" versus "upstream" endeavors:

> My friend, Irving Zola, relates the story of a physician trying to explain the dilemmas of the modern practice of medicine: "You know," he said, "sometimes it feels like this. There I am standing by the shore of a swiftly flowing river and I hear the cry of a drowning man. So I jump into the river, put my arms around him, pull him to shore and apply artificial respiration. Just when he begins to breathe, another cry for help. So back in the river again, reaching, pulling, applying, breathing, and then another yell. Again and again, without end, goes the sequence. You know, I am so busy jumping in, pulling them to shore, applying artificial respiration, that I have *no* time to see who the hell is upstream pushing them all in."

Evaluating the Content and Context of ▬▬▬▬▬▬
Education, Training, and Service Programs

For crisis trainers and administrators, the *Certification Standards Manual* represents a skeleton of standards, while this book adds substance to the bones in developing specific educational/training or service programs, evaluating their work, and preparing for national certification. The need exists for an exchange of ideas and strategies with people either contemplating new crisis training and service programs or wishing to evaluate their programs in light of others' experience and national standards. The remaining chapters address largely the *content* to be considered for such a developmental and evaluation process. Where content is not provided in detail, additional sources that trainers and program directors might find useful are suggested.

The task of evaluating the *context* of various education, training, and service programs is tailored much more to the unique needs and resources of individual settings and agencies. While *content* and *context* represent different aspects of a total process, they are dependent on one another. Thus, the core elements of a curriculum or crisis program (the *content*) can be identified and recognized nationally, while its distinctive features depend on the program's individual *context* and philosophy. These ideas are discussed in detail in Chapter 4.

The process of defining a "philosophy" is also necessary in developing service programs. The essential elements of a comprehensive crisis program—telephone, walk-in, outreach, and record-keeping—must be based on what the service providers (or board of directors) believe about crisis service, the community's needs, and particular obligations to meet these needs. Ideally, a program should be based on the characteristics and needs of particular communities. Thus, avenues for assuring this will vary from rural to urban settings and from suburban to inner-city areas while immediate access is a basic element.

ALICE SMITH ▬▬▬▬▬▬▬▬▬▬▬▬▬▬▬▬▬▬▬▬

In Centerville, a city of approximately 60,000, federal, state, and local funds support a community mental health center (CMHC). After 5:00 p.m. daily, professional staff are available by telephone only to any clients in crisis. As a consequence, some people in high-risk crisis states are referred to the police, and others go to hospital emergency rooms or seek support through a hotline staffed by lay volunteers from a church group. The volunteers and hospital staff receive no formal consultation, nor are there any interagency service agreements. Alice Smith, a client of the CMHC, calls her therapist after a heated argument with her husband over the weekend. Together they have been under stress from the threat of mortgage foreclosure on their farm. Alice is referred to the psychiatric service of the local hospital. There she receives a prescription for an anti-depressant drug and is told to see her CMHC therapist on Monday. The next day Mrs. Smith is brought to the same hospital emergency room after an overdose with her prescription pills.

One can speculate about several reasons for the state of affairs illustrated by this example (philosophy or beliefs influencing action):

1. The CMHC Board of Directors does not know about the essential elements and rationale for 24-hour, 7-days-a-week comprehensive crisis service.
2. Since the *volume* of acute crisis calls is perceived as small, the community is not convinced that it can support a comprehensive crisis service.
3. Professional staff of the CMHC have only sketchy knowledge of crisis service program development, which results in lack of coordination of existing services.
4. The community believes that traditional psychotherapy services are the most central to retain in an era of health care cost-containment, although this contradicts the original purposes outlined by federal legislation for community mental health (Levine, 1981).

As we evaluate the content and context of crisis training and service programs, we need to keep in mind that our objectives, content, and methods of training and service delivery flow from:

1. The nature of people in crisis.
2. The society or environment these people reside in.
3. The characteristics of the teaching/learning process.
4. The elements of the service delivery process.

These beliefs vary from person to person and in different cultural settings. But whatever the beliefs and values are, it is important to be explicit about them, as they will inevitably affect what is done for the client.

These contextual considerations imply several things. People contemplating a crisis education/training or service program need a thorough knowledge of the philosophy, needs, resources, and constraints operating in their educational or service agency and community. Also, if such knowledge is lacking, then the needs and resources must be assessed formally. This is a fundamental step in the planning process. Depending on political and other sensitive issues, a strategic step might be to contract with an outside, more objective source for the assessment.

References

Action for mental health. 1961. Report of the Joint Commission on Mental Illness and Health. New York: Basic Books.

Attorney General's Task Force on Family Violence. 1984. *Final report.* Washington, D.C.: U.S. Department of Justice.

Baldwin, B. A. 1975. "Alternative services, professional practice, and community mental health." *American Journal of Orthopsychiatry,* 45:734–743.

Bard, M. 1972. "Police family crisis intervention and conflict management: an action research analysis." Washington, D.C.: U.S. Department of Justice.

Bellah, R.N., et al. 1985. *Habits of the heart.* New York: Harper & Row.

Berman, A. 1983. "Survey of professional schools: Committee report to AAS board of directors." AAS Central Office: Denver, CO.

Burgess, A. W., and B. A. Baldwin. 1981. *Crisis theory and practice.* Englewood Cliffs, NY: Prentice-Hall.

Campbell, J., and J. Humphreys. 1984. *Nursing care of victims of violence.* Reston, VA: Reston Publishing Co.

Caplan, G. 1964. *Principles of preventive psychiatry.* New York: Basic Books.

Erikson, E. 1963. *Childhood and society.* New York: W. W. Norton.

Gibbs, L. 1982. *Love Canal—my story.* Albany: State University of New York Press.

Hoff, L. A. 1984a. *People in crisis: Understanding and helping.* 2nd ed. Menlo Park, CA: Addison-Wesley.

———. 1984b. *Violence against women: A social-cultural network analysis.* Ph.D. dissertation. Boston: Boston University.

———. 1987. The crisis model: Its centrality in primary health care and cost containment. Submitted to *Nursing Outlook.* February, 1987. (Adapted from paper presented at "Psychiatry in Africa and the Americas Today," Nairobi, Kenya, August, 1986.)

Levine, M. 1981. *The history and politics of community mental health.* New York: Oxford University Press.

Lifton, R. J. and E. Olson. 1976. "The human meaning of total disaster: The Buffalo Creek experience." *Psychiatry,* 39:1–18.

McKinlay, J. B. 1979. The case for re-focusing upstream: The political economy of illness. In *Patients, physicians, and illness.* 3rd ed. E. G. Jaco, ed. New York: Free Press.

President's Task Force on Victims of Crime. 1982. *Final report.* Washington, D.C.: U.S. Government Printing Office.

Surgeon General's Workshop on Violence and Public Health. 1986. *Final report.* Washington, D.C.: Health Resources and Services Administration (HRSA), U.S. Department of Public Health.

Wells, J. O., and L. A. Hoff. 1984. *Certification standards manual.* 3rd ed. Denver, CO: American Association of Suicidology.

2

Educational and Clinical Training Programs

STANDARDS FOR CRISIS TRAINING PROGRAMS

CORE CONTENT FOR EDUCATION/TRAINING IN CRISIS THEORY AND PRACTICE

Knowledge

Attitudes

Skills

QUALIFICATIONS OF CRISIS EDUCATORS AND TRAINERS

CONTINUING EDUCATION FOR CRISIS TRAINERS

CERTIFICATION OF CRISIS PRACTITIONERS

Standards for Crisis Training Programs ▬▬▬▬▬

Crisis training standards flow from the crisis field itself as a formalized body of knowledge and practice. The creation of such standards can be traced to three interrelated strands in the development of this service area:

1. The move during the 1960s to create alternatives to traditional health service delivery systems that would appeal to disaffected members of the community (Baldwin, 1975).
2. The beginning of the suicide prevention movement spearheaded by Edwin Shneidman and Norman Farberow (1957), a result of studying suicide notes.
3. The findings and recommendations of the 1961 Joint Commission on Mental Illness and Mental Health in the United States.

In spite of the Joint Commission recommendations and massive federal funding to support the development of 24-hour emergency mental health programs, it was largely volunteer citizen groups who responded to the need for such emergency services. However, reliance on volunteers' goodwill and intuition as a basis for practice was not enough, nor was a piecemeal approach to training sufficient to prepare volunteers for frontline crisis work. Similarly, professionals such as nurses, physicians, and social workers could rely no longer on their academic degrees alone to qualify them for helping people in crisis. Program administrators, crisis specialists, and licensed mental health professionals became concerned about wide disparities in training requirements and certain questionable practices in some training contexts (e.g., requesting trainees to role-play their own possible suicide without providing follow-up support).

In the early 1970s, these concerns were central to the movement and to the development of training standards for various workers in the crisis field. These standards are published in Area 2 of the *Certification Standards Manual* (the first edition released in 1976 with the fourth edition currently in process). In the 1980s, a parallel concern surfaced, to meet the special needs of people victimized by crime. Besides grassroots efforts such as the women's movement drawing attention to victims of rape and battering, three federal bodies focused on the neglected area of victims in crisis, the President's Task Force on Victims of Crime (1982), the Attorney General's Task Force on Family Violence (1984), and the Surgeon General's Workshop on Violence and Public Health (1986).

All three of these works highlight the fact that double victimization occurs because health and criminal justice professionals lack basic knowledge and skills in their work with victims, knowledge and skills that are common to crisis workers trained according to national standards. If people in crisis, including various victims of crime, are to receive the service they are entitled to, it is imperative that all health and human service workers are trained in the essential components of crisis theory and practice. At the Surgeon General's Workshop, members underscored this point in their *Final Report* by recommending that victimology and crisis intervention be included in the curricula and licensing examinations of all health and human service professionals.

In the remainder of this chapter, we outline CORE content in crisis theory and practice and elaborate on the various components of the training standards defined in the *Certification Standards Manual* (Wells and Hoff, 1984) that apply to volunteers or paid crisis workers in various crisis service programs. We also address the development of a certification program for individual crisis practitioners, lay or professional. In this discussion, we assume the common distinction between education and training. *Education* is associated with formal pre-service preparation of professionals in universities or colleges, and *training* refers to preparation or continuing education programs for those already employed (or anticipating employment—paid or volunteer) in a practice setting.

CORE Content for Education/Training in Crisis Theory and Practice

The notion of *CORE* content can be used in several different contexts. In formal pre-service professional programs—nursing, medicine, social work, and psychology—CORE crisis content would be part of a total curriculum. The term *curriculum* refers to the complex array of learning activities or a body of courses organized to achieve specific educational goals. *CORE curriculum* encompasses those courses required of all students graduating from an educational institution, without which the educational goals would not be met.

Moving to the course level, in this case a crisis course, *CORE* content refers to the **knowledge, attitudes,** and **skills** essential to any person practicing as a crisis worker, regardless of the setting or framework in which he or she learned this essential content. The concept of CORE content is important for several reasons. It emphasizes what every worker needs for managing complex crisis situations and avoiding inadvertent collusion in the process of double victimization. It also corrects the assumption that traditional curricula are enough without formal attention to recently developed crisis content. This is not to say that traditional curricula have totally ignored crisis content. But, recent trends toward primary health care and other developments (e.g., wholistic health care) suggest that disease models are inadequate to address contemporary problems like youth suicide and crises stemming from social problems such as hazardous waste disposal and victimization by crime or abuse. In addition, CORE crisis content enhances communication between various crisis service agencies and training units. Such communication avoids duplication of training and augments the trainees' sense of accomplishment around knowledge and skills already mastered. Thus, if a volunteer in a victim assistance program or other crisis service has successfully completed a four semester-credit crisis course with a clinical practicum conducted by a qualified instructor or trainer, she or he should not have to repeat the CORE content in an agency's training requirements. Rather, the volunteer could be examined on concepts from the CORE content, and the remaining time focused on application of this content to the unique circumstances of the employing agency. This recommendation also assumes the principles of adult education (Knowles, 1980; see Chapter 3, p. 49–52).

What, then, is this CORE content, and how was it identified as CORE? CORE crisis content falls into three categories, **knowledge, attitudes, skills.** These broad categories lay the foundation for objectives defined in terms that demonstrate acceptable **knowledge, attitudinal,** and **skill** outcomes. For example, a student can *identify* the steps of the crisis management process (**knowledge**), *demonstrate* in role-play a non-judgmental **attitude,** and *apply* the techniques of lethality assessment in a real or simulated case situation (**skill**). (These behaviorally defined outcomes or objectives are discussed in detail in the next chapter.)

The elements of CORE content were derived from the collective knowledge and experience of nationally and internationally recognized crisis specialists and suicidologists during the 1960s and 1970s. The development of crisis content in various professional programs was also stimulated by a proposal from the National Institute of Mental Health for a basic crisis curriculum and recommended reading lists in the field during this same period. This content was continuously refined through exchanges among experts at professional meetings and through evaluation of training programs by trainees, students, and trainer/educators in crisis settings around the United States and other countries. In the late 1970s and 1980s, various movements on behalf of victims (e.g., NOVA—National Organization for Victim Assistance, and battered women's groups) led to the inclusion of victimology in CORE crisis content (see Chapter 3 for details regarding implementation of CORE content).

Knowledge

Essential concepts that crisis workers must master include:

1. Crisis theory and principles of crisis management:

   - origins and development of crisis,
   - manifestations of crisis—emotional, cognitive, behavioral, and biophysical,
   - duration and outcomes of crisis, including effective and ineffective crisis coping,
   - steps of the crisis management process—assessment, planning, implementation, and evaluation,
   - application of the crisis management process to special groups at risk for crisis—drug abusers, victims of abuse, and the chronically mentally ill.

2. Suicidology, including principles of lethality assessment.
3. Victimology, including assessment of assault potential and victimization.
4. Death, dying, and grief work.
5. Principles of communication.
6. Ethical and legal issues regarding suicide, crime, and victimization.
7. Voluntary and involuntary hospitalization criteria.
8. Identification and use of community resources in crisis work.
9. Team relationships in crisis work.
10. The consultation process and its place in crisis management.
11. Principles and structures for record keeping.

As educators and trainers consider this CORE content, they must also evaluate the different approaches to this content taken by various writers. Serious attention to the theoretical underpinnings of crisis work is sometimes slighted since rapid action is often called for in crisis situations. It can also be cheated by students' and trainees' disinterest in theory and eagerness to get on to more practical concerns.

Since the original work of Caplan (1964), Lindemann (1944), and Erikson (1963), very few new theoretical approaches have been proposed to advance the crisis field. Exceptions to this include Taplin's (1971) work, Burgess and Baldwin's (1981) typology of six classes of crises, and Hoff's (1984a, 1984b) crisis paradigm based on research with battered women and application of the "life event" literature (e.g., Antonovsky, 1980) to clinical practice. This general deficit in the crisis field suggests the need for more conscious attention by practitioners to the theoretical foundations of their work.

For example, early work on child abuse was labelled as the "battered child syndrome" (Kempe, 1962). Basic to Kempe's "perpetrator-victim model" of etiology is the "syndrome" or physical examination findings in the child victim, which can be traced to the psychopathology of the parent-perpetrator. This focus flows logically from the history of medicine, which is heavily influenced by the philosophy of Descartes emphasizing mind-body separation. This philosophy supports the idea of "the body as a machine, of disease as a breakdown of the machine, and of the doctor's task as repair of the machine" (Engel, 1977:131). Descartes' dualistic philosophy is at least partially responsible for the general neglect of the social-psychological aspects of health and illness. In another belief system, abusive parents are viewed primarily as criminal, with the result that punishment, not treatment, is emphasized. The reality is more likely somewhere between these extremes and is complexly related to other contextual factors. Some abusive parents may be psychopathologically disturbed, but they are nevertheless influenced by a culture in which most people believe that *some* physical punishment is necessary for children, punishment that many may define as abusive and others as "normal." Also, although child abuse involves more than criminal activity, crisis workers dealing with parents are influenced by the legal mandate to report child abuse and protect the rights of children.

Educators and trainers also contribute to new theory development in the crisis field through thoughtful critique of the concepts proposed by writers to guide clinical practice. The major clinical texts outline in varying depth the general conceptual frameworks of their authors (Aguilera and Messick, 1986; Burgess and Baldwin, 1981; Hoff, 1984a; Janosik, 1984) (see Appendix A). Some texts rely heavily on general systems concepts while others are more socio-cultural and interactional in orientation (see Hoff, 1984a, pp. 9 –16 for an overview of theoretical influences on crisis theory). Educators and administrators need to examine critically the textbooks authors' conceptual frameworks and their implications for practice. Also, more research is needed to examine theory and practice and to build on the early concepts proposed by Caplan and Lindemann.

In general, the **knowledge** component of CORE crisis content is the easiest for students or trainees to master. Good textbooks, films, and students' willingness to read will complement classroom interaction with a creative teacher who elaborates, clarifies, and leads discussion and critique of the basic concepts (see Appendix B for a basic crisis library). The more challenging elements of CORE content for students and trainees to master are the **attitudes** and **skills** necessary for effective crisis work.

Attitudes

The CORE of crisis content includes these **attitudinal** outcomes of training:

1. Acceptance of and non-judgmental response to persons different from self and toward controversial issues, e.g., not discussing the moral rightness or wrongness of suicide or abortion with a person.
2. Balanced, realistic attitude toward oneself in the helper role, e.g., not expecting to "rescue" or "save" all potentially suicidal people or to solve all the problems of the distressed person, e.g., not expecting a battered woman to leave her abuser in spite of the fact that she may be unready because of obstacles she cannot overcome.
3. A realistic and humane approach to death, dying, self-destructive behavior, victimization, and other human issues, e.g., not asking questions of a battered victim like, "What did you do to provoke the beating?" or to a rape victim, not implying that she or he is at fault for having hitch-hiked.
4. Dealing with emotionally-laden issues like AIDS.
5. Coming to terms with one's own feelings about death, dying, and potential for violence, insofar as these feelings might deter one from helping others.

Teaching and training around these **attitudinal** issues require the trainer's continuous attention to his or her own attitudes and role-modeling open-mindedness to these sensitive issues. It also means realizing that helping people in distress is not a value-free endeavor. Attitudes will invariably be revealed in interaction between the crisis worker and the person in distress. Therefore, if a crisis trainer or clinician discovers that personal attitudes and beliefs will present a barrier to impartial and compassionate responses to people in crisis on controversial issues, it is best to acknowledge the problem and temporarily delay working with trainees or with clients.

It is important to note that rejection of clients or value-laden responses to them may arise from insufficient knowledge of the dynamics and ramifications of some crisis situations. For example, people who find it difficult to understand "why a battered woman stays," usually take another view of the issue when presented with the array of problems such a woman faces, problems much more complex than a superficial analysis reveals. However, people with inflexible views on controversial issues in society as a whole (e.g., abortion) are probably not suited for crisis work. For example, a person in crisis with AIDS has enough issues to face without the addition of judgmental attitudes from a crisis worker who believes that the disease is a deserved punishment for "immoral" behavior. In general, then, while the **attitudes** of some may remain fixed, new **knowledge** often results in the kind of flexibility necessary to assist people in crisis.

Skills

However, without certain **skills**, non-judgmental **attitudes** and thorough **knowledge** of concepts will not suffice. Trainees must be able to use their knowledge and attitudinal stance in a systematic, effective approach to particular people. An effective approach means assisting the person toward a crisis resolution consistent with the individual's values and meaning system. At the same time, a skilled crisis worker will help distressed people avoid negative outcomes of crisis such as violence, alcohol and other drug abuse, or chronic emotional or mental disability. Necessary **skills** to work effectively with people in crisis include:

1. Applying the techniques of formal crisis management—**assessment, planning, implementation, evaluation** (including assessment of victimization and risk of suicide and/or violence toward others).
2. Communicating—listen actively, question discretely, respond empathetically, and advise and direct appropriately.
3. Mobilizing community resources efficiently and effectively, e.g., engaging the rescue squad within 15 minutes of receiving a suicide attempt call, collaborating with the police in a violent situation without escalating the crisis and precipitating more violence, and making an appropriate referral for follow-up counseling or therapy.

4. Implementing policy and keeping records accurately and efficiently, e.g., recording essential notes in succinct form within the same workshift so they are useful to the next crisis worker.
5. Implementing the procedures for voluntary and involuntary hospitalization when indicated.
6. Using the consultative process, i.e., knowing *who* to call under *what* circumstances and in fact *doing* it.
7. Carrying out these crisis management steps while withholding judgment on controversial behaviors and not imposing values on the person in crisis and his or her family.

The minimum number of hours recommended by the American Association of Suicidology for achieving these **knowledge, attitudinal,** and **skill** outcomes is 40, 32 hours of classroom instruction and eight hours of supervised clinical practice. This is roughly equivalent to a four semester-credit college course. It is also similar to the training programs conducted by AAS certified crisis services in the United States. (In the next chapter we elaborate on time allocation in relation to CORE content, while application to different trainees and students is addressed in Chapter 4.) The ability to teach or train in a way that will result in these **knowledge, attitudinal,** and **skill** outcomes suggests an array of qualifications for the crisis trainer or educator.

Qualifications of Crisis Educators and Trainers

"Those who do not know how to do, teach; and those who do not know how to teach, consult." Professional educators and trainers for clinical practice have long struggled with the demands of teaching and training in a content area that demands the same work as of any other teacher, *plus* the requirement to keep up one's practice skills in rapidly developing clinical fields. Unlike education in theoretical disciplines, concepts in practice disciplines must be meaningfully linked to their application in the clinical field to maintain relevance to students and trainees. Not to do so results in the loss of students' attention and interest as well as the loss of teachers' credibility with students, in a word, teaching without knowing how to *do*.

The crisis field is no exception to this demand on clinical educators and trainers. In fact, the stress inherent in crisis work may be even greater than in less fast-paced practice fields. Crisis educators and trainers must manage to keep up their clinical practice skills in addition to the usual demands of teaching and training—content preparation, timely delivery, support of students/trainees, and evaluation of teaching methods and outcomes. Educators and clinical trainers who manage this dual challenge will do so more easily if they possess appropriate qualifications.

At the other extreme of teachers who lose credibility by falling behind in practice skills are those assuming that a skilled practitioner is automatically a skilled trainer. While some expert clinicians, with or without professional degrees, are also excellent trainers, there is no *necessary* equivalence between the skills required of clinicians and of teachers. To assume that there is suggests a devaluation of education as a distinct field requiring knowledge, attitudes, and skills different from those of clinicians. Of course, there are individuals who stand out for their clinical expertise *and* their ability to transmit CORE content in a highly effective manner (e.g., a person with special charisma). This combination of clinical and teaching expertise results from formal training in both areas with supervised practice by experts. What, then, does the formal preparation of qualified crisis trainers/educators consist of?

First, let us consider trainers working in health agencies or crisis programs' staff education and development positions. The *Certification Standards Manual* states that this person should have a *minimum* of "one year of supervised experience in crisis work . . . in which the prospective trainer demonstrates at least *above average* performance in the knowledge, attitudinal, and skill areas" discussed above. This evaluation of a prospective trainer is based on an agency's established criteria for satisfactory performance.

In addition, a trainer should have basic instruction in training methodology and techniques to:

- develop a course syllabus (objectives, content, methodology, evaluation, and bibliography),
- make appropriate bibliographical material available,
- develop lesson plans,
- develop or obtain audio-visual materials and other teaching aids,
- devise tests or other means of student/trainee evaluation,
- provide student/trainee support and direction,
- screen out and advise students/trainees who fail,
- develop systematic course evaluation plans as a basis for revision.

Ideally, an instructor's preparation includes work as a supervised co-trainer with an opportunity to discuss lesson plans and training problems. A properly prepared trainer will also arrange to be observed and evaluated by an experienced trainer.

In educational settings that prepare various health and human service professionals such as nurses and social workers, the faculty who teach crisis content should make themselves aware of the kinds of crisis training preparation discussed earlier. In addition, they should possess the same clinical performance ability as any clinical agency-based trainer. Such faculty members should have successfully completed at least one formal course in crisis theory and practice, or its equivalent in continuing education courses, in addition to formal qualifications in their particular practice disciplines for university or college teaching. (For trainers in service settings who are not required to meet basic faculty qualifications, we recommend at least some college preparation. Additionally, instructors and trainers might develop skills in the generic area of human relations through various training experiences such as the National Training Laboratory (NTL). Faculty should also recognize that a college degree or graduate degrees in mental health disciplines do not necessarily qualify people as crisis trainers.)

Because the crisis field has been recognized only recently as a distinct body of theory and practice, many would-be trainers and educators find themselves pressured to meet these requirements. Those working in areas where resources, especially experienced crisis trainers, are limited can seek creative alternatives that conform to the principles cited here. For example, an aspiring trainer could complete the following exercises for self-instruction:

- read several crisis textbooks for a thorough grasp of concepts and different theoretical approaches,
- take a local college course on educational psychology and/or teaching methods,
- arrange for an observation experience in a local emergency facility to broaden first-hand knowledge of crisis situations,
- arrange for a participant-observation experience with the local police department to broaden the trainer's experience with high-risk crisis situations and the realities of community integration for effective crisis work (such experience also expands the base of knowledge and experience for consultation in complex crisis situations),

- plan to attend national and regional conferences for gaining up-to-date information about the field and for networking with crisis experts,
- work as a volunteer or arrange a summer internship in a certified crisis service, preferably when a training course is being conducted (a list of certified crisis services is available from the AAS Central Office, 2459 South Ash, Denver, CO 80222; 303–692–0985).

Continuing Education for Crisis Trainers

Once crisis trainers or educators have met the basic requirements, the need to broaden and update their base of knowledge and refine their training skills continues. Many programs exist to meet this demand, as the necessity for continuing education in all health and human service professions is now widely recognized. In fact, licensed professionals (e.g., nurses and physicians) in some states are required to participate in a minimum number of continuing education hours to maintain their license to practice. While such legal requirements do not bind trainers, national training standards constitute a professional mandate to enhance their training skills through continuing education programs.

Educators preparing professionals in university programs have easy access to information about the many available programs. Also, a wide array of service agencies are on the mailing lists of university continuing education departments. However, individuals who need to attend these programs may not see the program announcements since they are usually sent to department heads. Or, the staff benefits program may not provide the necessary time and financial support for staff trainers to attend continuing education programs. If either is the case, enterprising trainers need to seek out these sources on their own.

In addition to universities' continuing education programs, there are a number of excellent curricula by the staff education divisions of well-established service agencies such as hospitals and certified crisis centers. National meetings provide another valuable avenue for continuing education. Each year, the American Association of Suicidology offers pre-convention workshops on various topics in the crisis field. Also, *Newslink,* the quarterly newsletter of the AAS, announces various continuing education curricula nationwide. Similar announcements are in the newsletter of the recently formed Task Force on Runaway Youth Suicide. Most of these programs include at least four-to-six hours of instruction. For more information about these programs, contact the American Association of Suicidology.

Also, trainers can plan more individualized experiences for themselves such as those suggested for basic qualifications. For example, a trainer needing more background in high-risk situations might arrange to observe some police training sessions along with a patrol ride-along experience. A trainer working in hospitals' staff development programs might attend the training sessions at a local crisis center with telephone hotline observation. Conversely, the crisis center trainer could attend staff development sessions with emergency room observation.

Exchanges like these would provide not only new information about training techniques and less familiar clinical cases, but also bridge some of the gaps and ease tensions existing between indigenous crisis services and traditional providers such as hospitals. For example, police officers often feel that their frontline crisis work is not valued by "professionals." But when professionals seek a training experience with the police, they give a message that nobody has all the answers; everybody has something to learn from each other, and that indeed, teamwork in crisis intervention is not only recommended, but often is a matter of life and death. While some people may fear the police patrol experience for safety reasons, it should be remembered that police officers take extraordinary precautions to protect civilians in these circumstances even though a release-from-responsibility signature is required. Trainers might also spend some time in one of the many shelters for the homeless, where over 50% of the clientele are deinstitutionalized mental patients, a high risk group who may use crisis hotlines.

Another newly developing source of continuing education is a Life Crisis Institute for Research, Education/Training, and Service at Northeastern University in Boston. This interdisciplinary Institute is co-sponsored by several university colleges and departments—nursing, health education, sociology/anthropology, counseling psychology, criminal justice, and allied health. Here, aspiring trainers receive formal instruction through trainer/training and other workshops conducted in collaboration with victim assistance programs and community mental health centers in the Metropolitan Boston area. The training opportunities available through this Institute include liaisons with certified crisis centers in the United States and Canada. For more information about this program contact: Lee Ann Hoff, Life Crisis Institute, Northeastern University, Boston, MA 02115; 617–437–3102.

Certification of Crisis Practitioners

Underpinning the certification of individual crisis practitioners are concerns similar to those that led to standards for crisis training in agencies. Since volunteers with no formal preparation in human service practice staff many of the indigenous crisis centers, quality control by employing agencies is still the basic issue. Thus, a certified crisis center assures the public that volunteers who staff these programs have met the minimum training requirements for crisis workers as defined by national standards. This includes a process to screen out training applicants who do not qualify.

Individual certification goes a few steps beyond these agency training program standards. Certification as a crisis worker follows the widely utilized certification practice among various professionals and organizations (e.g., physicians, nurses, psychologists, and alcoholism counselors). In these instances, certification signifies for example that a registered nurse with a master's degree (in addition to a general license, regulated by state legislators, to practice nursing) has met the special requirements of a "certified psychiatric nurse," controlled by professional organizations such as the ANA (American Nurses Association). Regarding the certification of crisis workers, the professional organization is the American Association of Suicidology, specifically, the Board of Examiners appointed by the AAS Board of Directors in collaboration with the Individual Certification Committee.

Certification thus attests to some basic ability on the part of the certificate holder. On the other hand, it does not *guarantee* high quality performance. Rather, it means that the certified individual has met or exceeded some fundamental test of probable ability and has achieved some basic level of knowledge, skill, experience, and ability to perform. This does not mean that the certified individual will be all things to all people or that a person is a superior being of some kind. Rather, certification offers consumers and employing agencies a vehicle to gauge better a person's *probable* performance possibilities.

Other advantages for the certified holder are status and prestige, particularly for those who, though very knowledgeable and skilled from years of training and experience, do not have other formal credentials such as an MSW or PhD degree. These benefits are especially prestigious in a culture where credentialing has taken on so much importance and consumers in crisis are vulnerable to questionable entrepreneurs whose major motivation is profit and not the provision of service. Individual certification also offers protection to consumers when there are pressures from certain political sources to develop services without the careful preparation demanded by national standards.

Although quality assurance to consumers is the major incentive for certification, those certified may also enjoy powerful market advantages. Within organizations, administrators may find that certified individuals are less costly to employ than volunteers or paid staff. For one thing, the certified person may require considerably less training, as there will obviously be some overlap between agency training standards and those applied to individuals.

Broadly, the requirements for individual certification as a crisis worker are

- AAS membership—regular or volunteer,
- successful completion of an approved training course,
- at least two years of clinical experience as a crisis worker, either full-time or a total of 500 hours.
- three references from persons directly familiar with the applicant's work,
- successful completion of a written and oral examination,
- satisfactory evaluation of clinical performance.

Policies and detailed procedures for this certification program are currently being completed and are expected to be operational by Fall, 1987. For further information contact the American Association of Suicidology.

References

Action for mental health. 1961. Report of the Joint Commission on Mental Illness and Health. New York: Basic Books.

Antonovsky, A. 1980. Health, stress and coping. San Francisco: Jossey-Bass.

Aguilera, D., and J. M. Messick. 1986. Crisis intervention. 4th ed. St. Louis: C. V. Mosby.

Attorney General's Task Force on Family Violence. 1984. Final report. Washington, D. C.: U. S. Department of Justice.

Baldwin, B. A. 1975. "Alternative services, professional practice, and community mental health." American Journal of Orthopsychiatry, 45:734–743.

Burgess, A. W., and B. A. Baldwin. 1981. Crisis theory and practice. Englewood Cliffs, NJ: Prentice-Hall.

Caplan, G. 1964. Principles of preventive psychiatry. New York: Basic Books.

Engel, G. L. 1977. "The need for a new medical model: A challenge for biomedicine." Science, 196:129–136.

Erikson, E. 1963. Childhood and society. New York: W. W. Norton.

Hoff, L. A. 1984a. People in crisis: Understanding and helping. 2nd ed. Menlo Park, CA: Addison-Wesley.

———.1984b. Violence against women: A social-cultural network analysis. Ph.D. dissertation. Boston: Boston University.

Janosik, E. H. 1984. Crisis counseling. Monterey, CA: Wadsworth Health Sciences Div.

Kempe, C. H., et al. 1962. "The battered child syndrome." Journal of American Medical Association, 181:17–24.

Knowles, M. S. 1980. The modern practice of adult education: From pedagogy to andragogy. Chicago: Association Press/Follett.

Lindemann, E. 1944. "The symptomatology and management of acute grief." American Journal of Psychiatry, 101:101–148. Also reprinted in Crisis intervention: Selected readings. H. J. Parad, ed. New York: Family Service Association of America, 1965.

President's Task Force on Victims of Crime. 1982. *Final report.* Washington, D.C.: U. S. Government Printing Office.

Shneidman, E. S., and N. L. Farberow, eds. 1957. *Clues to suicide.* New York: McGraw-Hill.

Surgeon General's Workshop on Violence and Public Health. 1986. *Final report.* Washington, D.C.: Health Resources and Services Administration (HRSA), U. S. Department of Public Health.

Taplin, J. R. 1971. "Crisis theory: Critique and reformulation." *Community Mental Health Journal,* 7:13–23.

Wells, J. O., and L. A. Hoff, eds. 1984. *Certification standards manual.* 3rd ed. Denver: American Association of Suicidology.

3

Implementing CORE Crisis Content

INTRODUCTION: THE DIVERSITY OF TRAINING GOALS

DEFINING OBJECTIVES IN BEHAVIORAL TERMS

CREATING A CLIMATE FOR TRAINING

IMPLEMENTING THE COURSE CONTENT—METHODOLOGIES

Lecture

Readings

Role-Play

Modeled Role-Play

CLINICAL PRACTICE FOR CRISIS TRAINEES

EVALUATING THE TRAINING PROCESS AND OUTCOMES

Introduction: The Diversity of Training Goals

The principles and methodologies discussed in this chapter apply to educators and trainers concerned with preparing crisis practitioners in educational or service settings. These include pre-service or continuing education programs conducted by a university- or college-based educator, a mental health professional, or a lay person specifically chosen for the task. Implicit in this discussion is recognition of the crossover between these various categories. For example, educators preparing students for eventual practice in any of the health and human service professions (nursing, social work, medicine, clinical psychology, and counseling) will conduct formal classroom sessions in the university setting, supervise the students' clinical experience in agencies providing crisis service (e.g., a crisis center or hospital), and hold seminars on clinical topics and experience in either the university or agency setting, whichever is available and/or more convenient to the students and instructors. Our discussion may also be relevant to educators in the various practice disciplines who conduct continuing education programs on crisis management for health and human service professionals. The trainees here are those who did not have crisis content in their pre-service programs or who wish to update their knowledge and skills. These programs vary widely in focus and extent, depending on the recipients' needs. Some of the most common formats are one- or two-day workshops or seminar series over several weeks (see Appendix B).

In general, this group of trainees do not function full-time as crisis workers. Rather, their knowledge and skill in the crisis field is incorporated into their regular practice as nurses, physicians, or psychotherapists. A psychotherapist trained in crisis management will feel confident, for example, in assisting the client or family during episodes of potential suicide or homocide. While in hospitals and home settings, crises associated with illness, accidental, and surgical loss, victimization or death are so commonplace that nurses and physicians untrained in crisis management often feel less than adequate in assisting such clients in crisis. For example, since 25% of pregnant women have a current or past experience of being battered by their mates, the importance of crisis assessment and referral of these women by nurses, midwives, and obstetricians cannot be sufficiently emphasized.

In contrast, the pre-service preparation of volunteer or paid staff in a crisis service (for the general population or distinct groups such as battered women or other victims of crime) occurs usually in the agency where the trainee will eventually work. Such training is conducted by an agency staff member with special preparation for this job or by outsiders with expertise in crisis training and sensitivity to the unique needs of the particular setting. Similarly, continuing education or in-service training of this group also takes place in the agency setting, though these workers may also take advantage of continuing education programs offered by a university or health agency.

Regardless of the focus (pre-service or in-service) or setting (educational or service), those facets of the education/training process that apply to all who encounter life crisis situations need to be highlighted. Training is not the same as teaching, and the design of crisis training programs is a highly specialized area of practice, involving small group skills, effective communication style, and other strategies foreign to both the mental health clinician and the educator whose experience is rooted in didactic learning. The crisis trainer must be willing to take risks and to model the integration of knowledge, attitudes, and skills required of a crisis worker.

The remainder of this chapter focuses on strategies dealing with the most challenging aspect of preparing crisis practitioners—the attitudes and skills required for dealing with sensitive issues and managing very stressful and sometimes life-threatening situations. This book emphasizes approaches to inculcate necessary knowledge that are more successful than the commonly used lecture method or "banking concept" of education, i.e., imparting large numbers of facts to trainees without integrating these facts with appropriate attitudes and skills. It is assumed that professional students, who are degree candidates in a health or other human service profession, will meet regular college and/or licensure requirements and require more theoretical and research underpinnings of crisis work. We emphasize the preparation for the *clinical* expertise needed by *all* crisis workers. Crisis specialists utilize continuously their preparation as crisis workers, while generalists integrate this preparation into another specialty area.

Defining Objectives in Behavioral Terms

The first step in a training program design is the development of clearly written objectives. These are most meaningfully stated in

behavioral or outcome terms, rather than in vague theoretical constructs. Objectives stated behaviorally provide both the trainee and
the trainer with a clear understanding of what is to be accomplished.
They define a task-oriented experience that provides for attitudinal
exploration, change, and growth. Furthermore, it is highly desirable
to frame the training objectives in measurable terms wherever possible.
This provides both trainer and trainee with clarity of expected
achievement. Too often broad statements like the following function
as objectives for crisis intervention training programs:

> "This class will provide the trainee with information about
> suicide risk assessment, crisis theory, and intervention
> strategies."

Clearly, this highly generalized description does not help the trainee
to understand what is to be mastered, nor the trainer to define a way
of measuring if, in fact, the content has been absorbed and integrated.
An objective stated behaviorally might include any of the following:

> "At the end of the third session, trainees will be able to
> identify five major factors in conducting a suicide risk
> assessment."

> "At the conclusion of the fourth session, the trainee will be
> able to define the agency's position on tracing calls as
> outlined in the Code of Ethics."

In effect, clearly stated objectives outline the content of the training
program. With this precise outline of the training format, the trainer
can determine the total amount of time to spend on the program.
This way, any time normally used to focus and refocus the objective
is eliminated, utilizing this additional time for constructive training.
Next, he or she defines the skeleton of the training program's basic
framework, the CORE content. Also, any content specific to the agency
or organization in its cultural and socio-economic setting needs to be
identified. Finally, the trainer determines the balance of time and
approach for adequate coverage of the material.

Appropriate textbooks or a notebook of selected reading material
are vital to the educational experience. Much of the didactic material
can be mastered through reading done on the trainee's own time,
organized so that each unit of reading material is completed prior to
the relevant session. Thus, classroom time can be used to review the

material, address special concerns, and practice assessment and intervention strategies through role-play, modeled intervention, and other training exercises (see Appendix C). It is also important to allow time for discussion of personal biases and attitudes as well as to process with trainees any feelings of distress that emerge from specific subject areas like suicide or AIDS.

Basically, the time assigned to different content areas should flow from the behaviorally-defined course objectives. Instructors can facilitate course planning by administering a pre-training questionnaire that identifies a learner's educational, training, and experiential background. Such information should guide the proportion of time allocated to the **knowledge, attitudinal,** and **skills** aspects of CORE content. It also contributes to the learner-centered instructional process that is so important in training around sensitive topics in the crisis field.

The training curriculum is clearest when objectives, content, and methodology are stated in relationship to each other. (In Appendix B, we present an excerpt from a course syllabus for "Crisis Workers in an Indigenous Agency" to illustrate the integration of objectives, content, and methods.) From these examples, we can observe the logical flow from stated objectives to content to methodology. Evaluation strategies for both trainees and the training program seem to construct themselves. There is also the clear possibility of developing a test for measuring the attainment of behavioral objectives, given prior to and on the completion of training. Such a test allows an evaluation of the trainee's mastery of the material and the impact of the training program as a whole. This becomes particularly important when the crisis program utilizes the skills of several different trainers at different times. It allows a measure of inter-trainer reliability by comparing the outcomes of one group with another and determining patterns of strengths and weaknesses.

Creating a Climate for Training

Training crisis workers (as for other clinical practice fields) is unlike most teaching experiences because a didactic approach alone cannot achieve the learning objectives set forth. The major instrument trainers use is an educated, secure self, which includes a high level of personal awareness, sensitivity, and objectivity; all are essential. Trainers must have a clear understanding of crisis theory, intervention strategies, and awareness of adult learning strategies (Knowles, 1980).

A crisis intervention training curriculum requires some initial time to create a climate of trust. This is true no matter who the trainees are—police, nursing students, hotline counselors, or any other population. Once trust is established, students/trainees will be willing to take learning risks, to examine their own biases, and to assist one another. The trainer must be willing to take the same risks as the trainees, e.g., to model role-plays to illustrate concepts addressed in lectures and readings. Learning occurs most effectively when the student participates actively in the learning experience. This is especially true when one is dealing with material that has potential emotional impact. The classroom becomes a laboratory for practice.

It is useful to communicate training policies at the beginning. These should be stated in terms of clear expectations with regard to attendance, participation, assignments, and other details. The structure of the training program may be described briefly. During this initial session (and in subsequent sessions) it is important to include opportunities for interaction between trainers and trainees because the emotional strength of the group collectively provides an encouraging atmosphere for trainees to take learning risks. There are numerous exercises to facilitate the building of an appropriate climate. One of the most effective is to ask the group to divide into pairs with someone unfamiliar, or at least not well-known, and to spend 15 minutes interviewing each other. If possible, the trainers should participate. When the time has elapsed, each person will introduce his or her partner to the group. This exercise has numerous benefits. It usually generates one supportive relationship in what may be a group of strangers. It can be utilized as an introductory exercise on the importance of listening and as a demonstration of how carefully we open up to strangers, even when we are not in crisis.

The importance of well-timed refreshment breaks should not be under-estimated. The ideal time in this first session is after the paired introductions. This allows people to pursue informally any conversation that they interrupted because of time constraints on the exercise. It also gives trainees a chance to converse about things they learned about each other in the introductions. This is the beginning of forging a group.

Other areas to include in the first session are

1. an exploration of the particular setting for training workers,
2. ethical considerations in crisis work with special emphasis on confidentiality concerns,
3. a discussion of the use of role-plays and appropriate feedback in the training program.

Each of these issues should be discussed in as participatory a way as possible. One might explore the particular setting by asking the group what they think the agency's business is about, what kinds of crises they anticipate working with, and what their experience has been. This approach helps to reveal the myths and realities of a given program and approach. The controlling philosophy of the community, the specific agency setting, and the personal models brought to crisis work are vital to acknowledge, understand, and possibly modify.

Throughout training, the trainer should utilize every opportunity to model basic attitudes desirable in crisis workers. The trainer who is shy, has poor communication skills, and lacks respect for people's abilities to cope or capacity for new learning, will not work successfully to help trainees develop as effective crisis workers. A skilled trainer allows trainees to anticipate certain experiences during each session through a clear statement in the written training objectives, content, and methodology.

Trainees should also be informed that they will be evaluated as fairly and objectively as possible and will be invited to evaluate the presentation and effectiveness of the program. Although the trainer becomes personally invested in the success of the group, it is vital to maintain an awareness that the well-being of the client is always the bottom line. If trainees demonstrate inappropriateness to crisis work, they will be given opportunities to address and change problem behavior or attitudes. But, if skills, knowledge, and desirable attitudes cannot be integrated, they may be asked to participate in some other area of work or to leave the program.

A discussion of ethical considerations is important at this early phase. The issue of confidentiality should be discussed from the perspective of the client and the group training experience because highly personal material will be introduced by some of the trainees, or somebody may have an unexpectedly intense reaction to particular content (e.g., suicide or rape) in the presence of other trainees. Also, throughout training the instructor may cite actual case material to illustrate and animate theoretical constructs. This is appropriate only after a clear and thorough discussion of confidentiality, and there is certainty of the group's awareness of the delicate and complex issues involved. Similarly, the ethical concerns and stances of the particular group must be acknowledged. For example, Child Protective Workers may operate under different ethical mandates than volunteer crisis telephone counselors regarding the reporting of possible child abuse to state authorities. Ethical issues will arise repeatedly, especially about interventions in high-risk situations. Thus, the trainer must be particularly sensitive to the anxiety these issues may generate.

Role-playing serves as a major training vehicle, so it is important to help trainees understand how to role-play, what kind of content is appropriate, and what their responsibilities are to each other for providing useful feedback. Some training manuals contain information about using role-play to maximum advantage. It is very helpful at this point for the trainers to model a brief role-play that contains both strengths and problems so that examples of helpful feedback can be provided for the group. Trainees should be instructed to avoid using current difficult personal problems that border on crises in their own lives for practice. Their "counselor" is most likely to be another novice crisis trainee, so there is probably no capacity for follow-up. To illustrate the theoretical constructs, it may be useful to prepare a number of suggested script outlines for use in each session, relating to the session content (e.g., a complex description of a current life situation for purposes of demonstrating lethality assessment). However, the scripts must be skeletal enough to demand from the trainees some emotional energy investment so that the role has meaning as a training strategy (see Appendix C for role-play situations).

The group should be encouraged to ask questions freely and express concerns as they surface. However, it is vital to have a reality check for the group because initial levels of anxiety may be high (what we have come to refer to as the "what-if " phenomenon, which can occupy endless amounts of class time with hypothetical discussions). Trainers need a good grasp of service program realities or should have an assistant who works with day-to-day aspects of program operations to contain these "what-ifs" within a reality-based context.

Another vital issue in crisis intervention training is the trainer's sensitivity to the experience of trainees. Ideally, a careful screening process should have taken place (see Chapter 7). This is certainly true for crisis intervention centers and suicide prevention programs (see Appendix C for pre-screening questionnaire). This is probably less true of classroom situations (e.g., nursing and medical school students) and police, so that one is less certain of the background and emotional stability that trainees bring. As noted earlier, even with careful screening, certain content areas may bring up uncomfortable issues that trainees thought they had fully resolved. Examples might be sessions focusing on alcoholic parents or domestic violence, issues that may have been carefully repressed. The trainer, therefore, must be alert to the responses of the group. Trainees who seem withdrawn or manifest signs of distress should be approached at the break or at the end of the session. Also, it is useful to let people know at the beginning that they may find themselves upset by a particular concern or aspect of training and to inform them of the resources available to share these concerns.

In our experience, even in a straightforward lecture on suicide prevention, there are frequently several people in the audience for whom the material raises serious concerns, reminders of past losses, or current problems. To accommodate this reality, it is always important to allow time for these concerns to be addressed. The spillage after class time also reveals that crisis work does not fit neatly into the traditional therapy hour, and that crisis workers must bring to their endeavors a high degree of flexibility and accessibility.

Implementing the Course Content—Methodologies

Crisis intervention training uses a number of modalities for instruction. These may include lecture, readings, role-play practice, modeled role-play (one of the most under-utilized and most valuable strategies), discussion, tapes and films, and other exercises. A well-designed training program will probably involve some of each. The pre-training questionnaire discussed earlier can alert an instructor to the methods and teaching styles trainers find most conducive to learning. In this section, we suggest some of the ways each method might be most useful. But whatever modalities are planned, the trainer should periodically assess with trainees their appropriateness for maximum achievement of learning objectives.

Lecture

This is perhaps the most over-used teaching approach found in training programs. Trainees should be able to absorb written concepts, content communicated through the written word in a training manual or a textbook. The trainer may wish to lecture about specific and vital areas such as lethality assessment and legal considerations in rescue. We recommend that lecturing be considered the method of last resort. But, when interactive learning is not possible through other means and there is essential content to be communicated, lecture may be the most efficient route.

Readings

There are several books available dealing with crisis intervention (see Appendix A). In addition, many certified crisis centers have developed their own training manuals, which include readings from a broad range of sources. Some are generic; others include information about specific areas of focus for the particular organization. Information about available training manuals can be obtained from the American Association of Suicidology. Certified crisis centers are particularly fruitful sources.

Role-play

Some of the concerns raised by role-playing have already been alluded to. Every AAS certified crisis center puts considerable emphasis on role-play as a central aspect of training. Whenever possible, it is helpful to have several trainers available to help small groups process role-plays. It is also useful to interrupt role-plays that are clearly going in the wrong direction and unlikely to straighten out. The role-playing "counselor" can be helped to see where the counseling contact derailed, what was overlooked (such as missed suicidal clues), and given the opportunity to try again.

Role-playing teams should contract to give each other honest feedback. Role-players often adopt an unspoken contract to state essentially the following:

> "I am the client, and I can feel you struggling in your role as the counselor. I feel uncomfortable to see you in such distress, so I will 'get well quickly' and tell you how helpful you have been to me."

Implicit in this message is the expectation that when roles are reversed the other person, in the role of client, will be equally generous. Trainees must be helped to see how vital honest feedback and consistency in role-playing are to their learning experience.

Modeled role-play

This technique demonstrates concepts and approaches. It is very helpful for example to model a role-play in which lethality assessment is conducted. Trainees with little or no experience in addressing the issue of suicide find it helpful to hear an experienced person ask directly about the client's self-destructive thoughts and behaviors. Trainers should be sensitive to any thematic difficulties that arise in the class and use demonstration role-plays to clarify problem issues. However, inexperienced trainees may be overwhelmed by the ease and competence with which trainers perform in role-plays. Their anxiety and need to identify special meanings and forms of self-expression should be addressed. They need to know that the trainers do not expect that upon completion of learning everyone will sound alike.

Even though discussion time is important, trainers should be wary of allowing it to continue for long periods of time. Role-playing often generates performance anxiety, and trainees may sabotage this part of training by diverting the trainer with questions and discussion. Similarly, training tapes and video can be utilized as supplements to training, rather than as substitutes for experiential learning. Tapes are very useful when it is important to have control over the client part of the role-play for purposes of demonstration, for example, modeling a response to a sexually exploitive caller to a crisis service. Role-play techniques are also highly recommended for the development of communication skills. All crisis workers need to learn basic communication skills—active listening, the use of open-ended questions except when there is the clear need for immediate and concise information, clarification, gentle confrontation, etc. There are numerous articles and books useful in designing a communication skills unit (see Appendix A). In addition, many crisis centers include communication skills material in their training manuals. Finally, every crisis educator and trainer should take advantage of the rich, up-to-date training resources available through the SIEC (Suicide Information and Education Center). The SIEC is a computer-assisted resource library containing written and audio-visual materials specific to the topic of suicidal behaviors and crisis intervention. The address of SIEC is Suite 103, 723–14th Street N.W., Calgary, Alberta, Canada T2N 2A4; 403–283–3031.

Clinical Practice for Crisis Trainees

An apprentice period is a significant phase of training. Trainees should not be expected to apply the principles and techniques of the classroom in real life situations without the support and supervision of a skilled crisis practitioner, either the trainer or someone designated for that function. Such apprenticeship periods must be formally planned, lest the trainee's need for supervision be left to chance. Thus, the pairing of trainees with experienced crisis workers plays a vital role in the trainees' education.

Experienced crisis workers help trainees process actual contacts they have observed, explain why certain decisions were made, analyze the process of the contact, and answer any questions trainees have. This, however, puts considerable pressure on the experienced worker because trainees emerge from their learning experience with the material fresh in their minds and clear notions of the "right" way to do things. This may be threatening to the experienced worker slightly out-of-touch with the formal aspects of his or her own training. The worker may also feel microscopically observed and needs to have a clear understanding of her or his role in helping people through the apprentice periods.

In addition, the experienced worker's role in evaluating the trainee should be clearly stated and understood. As trainers select various methodologies to use in crisis training, they may find it useful to consider the principles of self-directed learning that apply especially to adult learners. The term "andragogy" has come to be associated with the needs of adult learners. It originates from the Greek word 'aner' (meaning adult) and describes the body of theory and practice on which *self-directed* learning is based. It is thus defined as the art and science of helping adults (or, even better, maturing human beings) learn. In contrast, the body of theory and practice on which *teacher-directed* learning is based is often given the label "pedagogy," from the Greek words 'peid' (meaning child) and 'egogus' (meaning guide or leader), defining it as the art and science of teaching children.

These two models do not represent good/bad or adult/child dichotomies, but rather a continuum of assumptions to be evaluated in terms of their appropriateness for learners in particular situations. If a pedagogical assumption is realistic for particular circumstances, then pedagogical strategies are appropriate. For example, if certain crisis content areas are entirely new and strange to a learner, he or she will be dependent on a teacher until enough content has been acquired to enable self-directed inquiry to begin. However, even in an essential content area such as assessment for suicide risk, which entails research-based knowledge and particular techniques, a learner-centered process is recommended. For example, since everyone has ideas about why people commit suicide—some accurate and some misguided—these ideas can be elicited from trainees as a way to activate them in the learning process and help dislodge common myths such as "talking directly with people about suicide puts the idea into their heads." As noted earlier, an interactive approach is more effective than other training methods for sensitive topics in the crisis field because of the learner's increased involvement. These ideas are summarized in Figure 3.1 (Knowles, 1978, 1980, 1975). To avoid gender bias in language, we suggest the term "collaborative" as a substitute for Knowles' "andragogical" model of learning as illustrated in Figures 3.1b and 3.1d.

Evaluating the Training Process and Outcomes

Crisis programs utilize a number of strategies for evaluating the impact of training. One particularly effective approach is the administration of a test before and after training. Such a test can measure, through objective questions, the trainee's knowledge of crucial areas such as risk assessment, legal and ethical considerations, and basic counseling approaches. A number of instruments are available (see Appendix C). Subjective evaluation of trainee performance is a valid part of the process; however, it is vital to have clear criteria for evaluation. This may be done by a final role-play with the trainee observed for the integration of knowledge, attitudes, and skills.

Trainees should be given the opportunity to evaluate their training experience, either after each session or at the completion of the course, and once again a few months later when they have been working in a crisis intervention setting. Furthermore, it is important for the agency to communicate the seriousness with which such evaluations are viewed. These evaluations should be utilized to revise and redesign training approaches when thematic difficulties or areas for improvement emerge from the trainee's experience and suggestions. In addition to trainees' evaluations, it is highly desirable to assess the effectiveness of training based on its impact on the clients served by those trained. Such assessments, however, need to be complemented by independent judges of the client's functioning (Stein and Lambert, 1984:121–123; Hornblow and Sloane, 1980:137, 377–378; Pearce and Snortum, 1983:71–92). This type of evaluation usually requires formal assistance from professionals trained in evaluation research methods. Agencies should seek out such sources to supplement the in-house evaluation methods that are an ideal of every training program.

Figure 3.1a

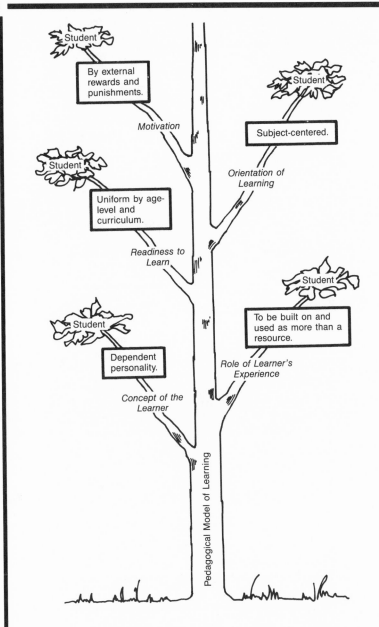

Assumptions about learning and the learner: The Pedagogical Models. Implies hierarchical relationship between teacher and learner.

Figure 3.1b

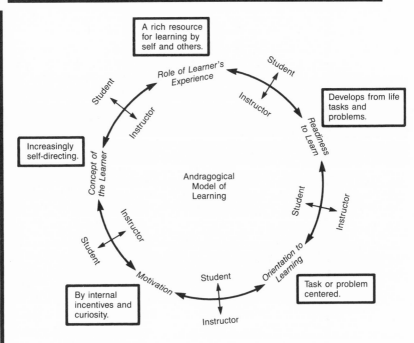

Assumptions about learning and the learner: The Andragogical Model. Implies interactional relationship between learner and teacher.

Figure 3.1c

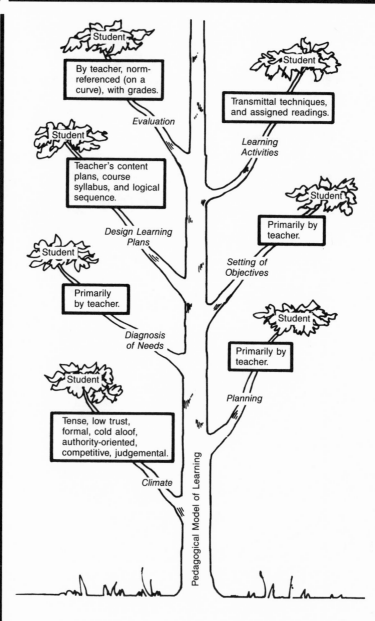

Elements of the teaching-learning *process*: The Pedagogical Model.

Figure 3.1d

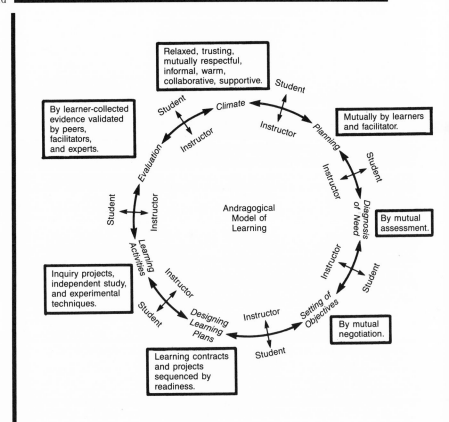

Elements of the teaching-learning *process*: The Andragogical Model.

References

Hornblow, A. R., and H. Sloane. 1980. "Evaluating the effectiveness of a telephone counseling service." *British Journal of Psychiatry,* 137:377–378.

Knowles, Malcolm S. 1975. *Self-directed learning: A guide for learners and teacher.* Chicago: Association Press/Follett.

————. 1978. *The adult learner: A neglected species.* 2nd ed. Houston: Gulf Publishing Co.

————. 1980. *The modern practice of adult education: From pedagogy to andragogy.* Chicago: Association Press/Follett.

Pearce, J. B., and J. R. Snortum. 1983. "Police effectiveness in handling disturbance calls: An evaluation of crisis intervention training." *Criminal Justice and Behavior,* 10(1):71–92.

Stein, D. M., and M. J. Lambert. 1984. "Telephone counseling and crisis intervention: A review." *American Journal of Community Psychology,* 12(1): 101–126.

4

Differential
Application of
CORE Content

INTRODUCTION

COMMUNITY AND CULTURAL CONTEXT OF
CRISIS TRAINING

ASSESSING ATTITUDES, BACKGROUND, AND
NEEDS OF TRAINEES

TAILORING A TRAINING PROGRAM IN
INTERACTION WITH TRAINEES

IN-SERVICE TRAINING OR CONTINUING
EDUCATION PROGRAMS

COMMUNITY GATEKEEPERS' TRAINING

Introduction

The range of people for whom crisis training is relevant and crucial includes a broad spectrum of health and human service workers — firefighters, child abuse workers, clergy, physicians, nurses, allied health workers, law enforcement officers, mental health professionals, and others. In addition, crisis training is important for gatekeepers — teachers, bartenders, telephone operators, disc jockeys, beauticians, Traveler's Aid workers, and anyone else who encounters people on the frontlines, in a pre-crisis state, in a life or death situation, or in a deteriorating state of mental health. Thus, because of the broad spectrum of crisis workers, the contextual factors and unique needs to master and integrate the knowledge, attitudes, and skills for effective crisis work must be considered. Chapter 4 explores some of the differential training implications for people in these groups.

Emphasis is placed on general principles that might guide professional educators and agency-based crisis trainers in designing programs that fit the needs of particular students and trainees. Implicit in this discussion is the CORE content, which will vary in focus, depending on the needs of trainees and the theoretical framework of the individual educator or trainer. To supplement these general guidelines, Appendix B contains samples of course syllabi and continuing education programs to illustrate in greater detail the application of CORE crisis content to various groups (e.g., university students in the health professions, practicing crisis workers (full- and part-time), police, and victim advocates).

Community and Cultural Context of Crisis Training

The content and shape of the training material will be somewhat controlled by the setting and community in which training is offered and the staff for whom it is provided. While CORE content is always included, working with home health aides in a rural community, for example, involves a different psychosocial milieu and probable concerns than training police officers in a large metropolitan area. This may seem absurdly self-evident; yet, it is a fact that many small town police staffs are trained as if being prepared for intervention in urban gang warfare, when in reality their work will focus primarily on social service. A police officer in a small community is likely to work with ten times as many suicidal people as with victims of armed robberies; yet, officers are probably provided with only skeletal training in working with suicidal and emotionally distressed individuals.

Another distinction to keep in mind is the community's general access to resources and technological development. For example, training in CORE crisis content for health aides on a Native American reservation or for village health workers in Kenya will be strongly influenced by crises in these settings that stem from poverty and the lack of resources that people in industrialized societies take for granted. In addition, there are cultural factors to consider when designing any training program. These may include linguistic barriers and different cultural values regarding issues like personal privacy, gender expectations, extended family networks, differential living situations, and other culturally defined patterns. Working against deeply held cultural values may condemn crisis intervention efforts to failure; at the same time, one must not make assumptions based on cultural myths. An example might be the belief that "violence against women is just part of that group; women expect it and accept it."

In the early stages of a generic crisis intervention program's development, it is vital to conduct a community needs assessment to determine the nature of the psychosocial problems likely to surface. These will probably always include domestic violence, rape, suicide, sexual identity concerns, alcoholism, developmental problems, and drug abuse. However, the setting also determines the type of problems to arise. A particular area may suffer from the stressors of periodic unemployment because a major employer shuts down for periods of time, or of permanent unemployment because a major industry leaves the community. Similarly, a region subject to periodic flooding or earthquake has needs determined by the hazardous environment. An area with substantial minority populations struggles more overtly with issues of racism. In other words, program planners need a working knowledge of the types of crisis-provoking situations to which workers may be called upon to respond. A variety of strategies for assessing the needs of the community in relation to overall crisis program planning are discussed in Chapter 5. These needs should be reflected in training.

Assessing Attitudes, Background, and Needs of Trainees

Not only is the content of the program controlled by the context, but the nature of the training is shaped by the needs and background of the participants (Hoge and Hirschman, 1984). In teaching the basic steps of crisis management—assessment, planning, implementation, and follow-up—there will be contextual differences specific to the trainees or students who may be police officers, nurses in a psychiatric master's degree program, or lay volunteers for a crisis hotline, victim assistance program, or battered women's shelter. This is why general principles and various examples are presented, but the notion of a single over-arching model is avoided. For example, in a baccalaureate nursing program, crisis content might be taught around these key concepts in a nursing curriculum—person, environment, health, and nursing. That is, a *person* may experience an emotional crisis state as a result of being raped in a cultural *environment* generally not safe for women alone at night. Depending on the *help* received by the rape victim (from *nurses* or others), her *health* status may be negatively affected by this experience.

Both undergraduate and graduate students will need more theoretical underpinnings if their study of crisis management is part of academic coursework. On the other hand, since graduate students in the mental health professions have generally mastered the basics of communication skills central to all human service work, they usually need less emphasis on this content area than police officers or paramedics, for example. Similarly, the level of psychological complexity in the content will be different in the preparation of psychiatric residents or nurses than emergency medical technicians. The program should be tailored to the participants' abilities and requirements, to knowledge and skills already mastered, and to the realities of potential clients. It is also important to make the content substantial enough to provide sufficient intellectual and emotional challenge.

Trainers must also consider the biases they might encounter with a particular training group. Medical students may bring a deep commitment to in-office or in-hospital care, to the notion of people who need help as patients, and to a model of illness and cure. If so, this bias must be openly addressed and challenged in a non-hostile manner if the crisis training is to be effective. Adequate information is the best response to such a bias. The trainer should also have a thorough and communicable knowledge of crisis theory with a deeply held personal belief in the provision of help in the least restrictive setting possible in any given situation (often this translates to a community setting or the person's home). If the focus of the agency is on domestic violence, trainers must ascertain whether participants carry some of the prevalent attitudes toward battered women, for example. Many people believe a battered woman is probably the cause of violence, she brings it on herself, if she really wanted to get out she would, or, most invidious of all, she really enjoys it.

In addition, it is important to emphasize the differences between crisis intervention and substantially different approaches to working with people whose training and experience may be in conflict with a crisis approach (see Hoff, 1984a: 20–21 for details of how crisis intervention differs from related human service functions). For example, the mental health professional may immediately begin the process by taking a case history. The police officer may fire questions and look for quick solutions. It is then especially helpful to ask one of the trainees early in the curriculum to role-play a crisis situation and to respond as naturally as possible within his or her usual mode of response. This can be followed by a modeled role-play of the same situation in which the principles of crisis management guide the process and outcome. Such a strategy can form a useful and dramatic basis for group discussion.

The type of training manual or text used will be controlled by the context of the training program, the instructor's theoretical framework, and the educational level of the participants. Assessment information, crisis theory, intervention strategies, operational and procedural guidelines, a code of ethics, and sample forms should be part of any training material. A manual that reinforces basic concepts of crisis intervention and management, whatever the special focus of the program, cannot be sufficiently stressed. However, if one is training advocates to work with battered women, for example, one might assign additional material such as excerpts from the book, *Getting Free: A Handbook for Women in Abusive Relationships* (NiCarthy, 1982); whereas, if one is training crisis workers who are prison advocates, the suggested range of readings might include *Crisis Behind Bars* (Danto, 1981).

In other words, the application of crisis theory and intervention to a specific population group enlivens what might otherwise seem too general for crisis workers who are in a focused setting. For example, sharing information about the reality of battered women is helpful to trainee advocates for battered women. They realize that many, if not most, women in battering situations have, at times, some suicidal feelings. Also, a substantial number of such women have acted on these feelings because a suicide attempt may seem like an easier way to escape a violent relationship than their other options. This kind of example dramatically emphasizes the need for training in lethality assessment within the context of an experience to which trainees can relate.

Tailoring a Training Program in Interaction with Trainees

If crisis training is provided for the staff of a program already in operation, it is important to develop a data collection mechanism enabling the training program to be tailored to the real demands placed on workers. The training designer should involve workers through interviews and questionnaires that indicate the nature of their experience, areas in which they feel the need for crisis training, and other relevant issues. This will provide a sense of ownership by those participating in the training and will reduce resistance and skepticism by people who feel that they "know it already." An example might be providing training for case managers who work with the mentally ill once they are released from institutional care. These are frontline workers, subject to a great deal of stress from a high-risk population, a too-heavy caseload, frequent inability to summon support from the psychiatric community when needed, and often too little pay. To be effective, a crisis program must relate directly and concretely to the nature of the stressors of their work and must recognize what they already know. Training can be offered as a way of helping them to be more effective, less dependent on outside "experts" to get a client through a period of crisis, and more certain about their ability to make assessments.

Similarly, the program must recognize the stresses of police work, for example. The trainer must acknowledge that some police officers are killed intervening in domestic situations, sometimes because they lack the crisis intervention needed to conduct these interventions more safely and effectively (Crego and Crego, 1983). This approach forges an alliance between the trainer and the trainees. When possible, it is useful to use an indigenous trainer, involve a trained police officer to work with law enforcement personnel, a physician trained in crisis intervention to work with medical students, a nurse to work with nursing students, etc. But, the reality is that too often this is not possible; therefore, it may be useful to forge an alliance with an indigenous staff member and make that person a working assistant in doing demonstration role-plays and other parts of the training.

The trainer needs to be sensitive to particular forms of resistance in some aspects of training by certain groups. Some mental health professionals may be reluctant to participate in role-plays. Police officers may be uneasy about guided fantasy exercises. Sometimes modeling by the trainer will help to overcome resistance; however, one needs to be alert to the reactions of the group and not get locked into a combative position. Flexibility is required to shift to another mode when this resistance is extreme.

In-service Training or Continuing Education Programs

The continuing education needs of mainstream health workers (e.g., nurses and physicians) is determined by the extent and depth of CORE crisis content in their generic program or pre-service preparation and by new developments in the field such as the recent emphasis on victimology content for all licensed health workers (Surgeon General, 1986). In general, CORE content needs to be adapted to the background of these professionals and to their current needs.

At the conclusion of pre-service training for all groups, it should be made clear to trainees that they have only begun their learning experience. On-going training is essential for the continued growth of the crisis worker. In addition, in-service education reinforces skills and concepts marginally mastered during the initial training. AAS Certification Standards require a minimum of six hours per year of mandatory in-service training for staff (volunteer or paid) of certified crisis programs. Many agencies offer excellent in-service programs; however, some are not sufficiently rigorous about requiring attendance, particularly of their volunteers. Yet, volunteers have the same obligations and expectations as paid workers; they are simply paid in a different currency.

In general, in-service training requirements are determined by program context in the same way as pre-service training design. One of the most useful ways to assess in-service training needs is with a questionnaire after the trainee has completed three to six months of post-training service. The worker is then in a position to comment on how well training equipped her or him for the actual work, areas of training that need reinforcement or were not covered at all, concerns raised by clinical field work, and other issues that emerge. This evaluation can be used to plan in-service training sessions. We have found that the most effective program balances *informational* sessions (speakers from outside agencies who describe the work and function of their programs, or who address special concerns such as AIDS) with *experiential,* skill-oriented sessions (reviewing lethality assessment through role-plays and developing advanced counseling techniques).

Continuing education programs are often in-house; but, there are other options, depending on the locale and the resources of the agency. Many of these are similar to those suggested for instructors in Chapter 2. It may be possible for people to attend regional, state-wide, or national meetings to update knowledge of crisis theory and practice. Each year before its national convention, the AAS, for example, conducts a continuing education program on some aspect of crisis work. In addition, audio cassette tapes now serve as training tools. Many of these are available through university libraries. Some agencies may wish to make their own video or audio tapes for in-service training. Periodic refresher courses are useful. One agency conducts what has affectionately come to be known as "retread training," a 12-hour mandatory refresher course given to volunteer staff every second year.

Agency personnel may wish to look elsewhere in the community for ongoing training. It may be useful for some of the staff to take Emergency Medical Technician training under the local Red Cross. Others who are preparing to move up to a supervisory level can participate in a course on supervision at a local institute or social work program. A cooperative relationship with other mental health services will facilitate co-sponsorship of in-service programs and notification when other agencies are providing workshops. Most crisis programs offer opportunities for workers to move up in responsibility. This professional development is important for both paid staff and volunteers. Line workers may move to supervisory positions, may become trainers, or may assist by conducting pre-service interviews. The agency must provide adequate training for these new responsibilities.

Community Gatekeepers' Training ▰▰▰▰▰▰▰▰▰

Community "gatekeepers" are persons who frequently encounter people in crisis, but whose primary role is not crisis intervention service. These gatekeepers include bartenders, disc jockeys, teachers, and telephone operators. The training for these community groups is based on two premises. First, most people accept the AAS slogan that "suicide prevention is everybody's business," and that every citizen is obliged on humanitarian grounds to assist fellow human beings victimized by crime or for whatever reasons they are in acute distress. Second, the work of gatekeepers or any citizen will be less stressful and scary if their skill as "natural crisis managers" is enhanced by the basics of how to assess risk of suicide or violence, how to use resources, and how to make an appropriate referral. For example, in many cases of suicide, tragedy might have been avoided if ordinary family members were more aware of the common indicators of life-threatening behavior. The goal, then, is not to remake these gatekeepers into regular crisis counselors, but to reduce their stress by providing them the knowledge and skills necessary to link distressed people to professional crisis services.

In short, the education needs of gatekeepers and the general public in the basics of crisis intervention can be compared to campaigns regarding cancer detection, AIDS, and the dangers of smoking. The focus is on detection, empathic response, and appropriate referral to crisis specialists. This kind of training is also referred to as "community education." The distinction between training for these groups, mainstream health and human service workers, and the role of crisis specialists is illustrated further in Chapter 8.

References

Crego, C. A., and M. W. Crego. 1983. A training/consultation model of crisis intervention with law enforcement officers. In Cohen, L. H., W. L. Claiborn, and G. A. Specter., eds. *Crisis intervention* (pp. 71–88). New York: Human Sciences Press.

Danto, B. 1981. *Crisis behind bars: The suicidal inmate. A book for police and correctional officers.* Warren, MI: Dale Corporation.

Hoff, L. A. 1984a. *People in crisis.* 2nd ed. Menlo Park, CA: Addison-Wesley.

Hoge, M. A., and R. Hirschman. 1984. "Psychological training of emergency medical technicians: An evaluation." *American Journal of Community Psychology,* 12(1):127–131.

NiCarthy, G. 1982. *Getting free: A handbook for women in abusive relationships.* Seattle: Seal Press.

Surgeon General. 1986. *Report: Workshop on violence and public health.* Washington, D.C.: U.S. Department of Public Health (HHS).

5

Planning and Developing Crisis Programs

Introduction

Crisis intervention programs have proliferated in recent years. There are rape crisis programs, crisis centers for battered women, and suicide prevention programs that often expand into crisis intervention services. In fact, studies reveal that many of the callers to suicide prevention centers are not suicidal, but call to discuss a crisis or a personal problem. It is not appropriate to apply the term crisis service to a program operating within traditional constraints, open from 9:00 a.m. to 5:00 p.m. and office-bound. Crisis services must be available 24-hours a day, every day of the year, must be immediately accessible, and must be well-publicized and clearly understood by the community the program serves. Thus, it is crucial that the planners, developers, and implementers of a crisis program understand fully the nature of the service they undertake to provide.

The work of a crisis center may reflect the community's pulse by rendering an early reading of its special stresses, fears, social problems, and needs. It is the responsibility of a crisis center to take an activist position in community planning for services. For example, in Ithaca, New York, the crisis service became acutely aware of the lack of emergency shelter because crisis workers spent many hours attempting to locate resources to house clients. Careful records were maintained and the center played a central role in community planning meetings that resulted in a task force to develop an emergency community shelter. This kind of participation requires a sensitive and far-sighted board of directors that sees the role of the crisis center in the community as not only working with clients in crisis, but also treating the entire community as a client with potentially crisis-inducing social problems. Therefore, a board of directors plays a central role in the direction and impact of any crisis program.

Board Selection

Many crisis intervention programs exist as free-standing agencies managed by a board of directors. Some are programs of a larger organization, like the emergency service unit of a community mental health center. Still others may be a component of a mental health clinic. (These differing models are discussed further in the next chapter.) Whatever the arrangement, the board plays a vital role in the functioning and oversight of the crisis program. Some agencies utilizing volunteer crisis workers do not permit them to serve on the board. Others may have boards comprised entirely of crisis workers. Many have settled on a compromise position and have some volunteer representation on the board. Regardless of composition, the board of directors is legally accountable for the conduct, services, and financial stability of the agency. Therefore, most boards avail themselves of legal services by purchasing malpractice insurance to protect staff and the agency in their service role to the public.

Careful selection of members is vital to the smooth and effective operation of the board. It is useful to maintain a balance between people knowledgeable in the areas of financial management and resources, personnel management, mental health service providers, and volunteers and interested citizens. While many boards like to involve prominent members of the community (e.g., bank presidents and corporation directors), these individuals are usually so overcommitted that they are able to contribute little more than their names to the board. A working board might better be comprised of the manager of a branch bank, a new attorney in the process of establishing a private practice, a personnel administrative assistant, and others who have the time, energy, and commitment agencies need from their directors. If the agency wishes to involve the community's prominent people, invite them to join an *ad hoc* advisory committee or to function as consultants in the area of their expertise.

In addition to these factors, the focus of the agency and the community's special nature should influence board selection. For example, if a program is targeting adolescents, a representative of the school system will be a useful board member. For most crisis programs, a working relationship with the police or other law enforcement agency is essential; it will probably be helpful to have a respected member of that agency on the board. If the community has a substantial sub-population, e.g., a college town, someone from the sub-population will be an important board connection. Politically, it may be advisable to invite a board membership to a representative from an agency or organization that plays a key role in the smooth functioning of the service program, such as an administrator from the Department of Social Services or a representative from a major mental health agency. In addition, if relations with an agency that are vital to the program's smooth operation have been problematic, inviting a representative from that agency will help to work through difficulties.

Whenever there is board turnover, if at regular election time or when there has been an appointed or elected substitute to fill an empty slot, an orientation is vital. This should be conducted by the agency's executive director as well as by the board president, and it should include:

- an overview of the agency and its programs and staffing pattern, including an explanation of the organizational chart,
- a brief history of the agency,
- an explanation of the annual budget—income sources and expenditures as well as an explanation of how the board monitors the agency's fiscal position,
- a description of the board's committee structure,
- a tour of the facility.

In addition, new board members should receive packets of information with the most recent annual report, financial statements, board minutes, list of the full board and staff names and positions, brochures, and other material describing the agency's work. The United Way of America has prepared several excellent documents regarding board participation, responsibility, and liability. Local United Way agencies can be contacted for the address to obtain these materials.

Board business is often conducted in committees, with the full board receiving reports from the committees, and with ample time for discussion and questions of committee recommendations. A working board membership is a substantial time commitment, and it is only fair to both the agency and the potential board member to state initially what the commitment comprises. For most boards, this involves at least two meetings a month, the regular monthly board meeting and a committee meeting. It is also useful to enforce the board's policy of requiring members who miss a certain number of meetings to resign. Too many boards carry members in name only from year to year. The seat of the absent member might well be succeeded by a highly-involved and energetic person.

Funding

In this era of shrinking public money, funding for crisis programs is almost always problematic. There are both public and private models as well as combinations of the two. Some probable resources include a contract with the state's Department of Mental Hygiene or its equivalent, a contract with the local county government to provide crisis services, United Way funding (which is seldom the sole source of support for any of its agencies), and special funding for targeted programs within the agency, such as a division for youth monies for parts of the program directed toward young people. Some funding sources, especially state agencies, provide matching funding; the agency can receive up to a certain funding ceiling, provided it can match the dollars from other non-state sources such as private fundraising efforts, contributions, and the United Way. This presents an effective argument for seeking donations because each contributed dollar generates another dollar from the public sector. In addition, it may be possible to arrange a contract with one of the local hospitals.

Start-up funds may be obtained through a local foundation, but it is vital to have a plan for continued funding at the time of application. Local foundation resources can be located through the United Way, other human service planning departments, or by a search through the library's foundation directories. If there is a university nearby, personnel from the development office may be helpful in identifying local foundations interested in human services.

Most agencies will have to conduct some sort of fundraising. Possibilities include membership campaigns and events like garage sales, book sales, or entertainment evenings. These events heighten the agency's visibility in the community and strengthen the sense of commitment and involvement among those planning and implementing them. But, they may also generate burnout by placing too many demands on people whose skill and time are needed to provide service or to monitor the event from the board. A careful balance must be struck. Direct appeals to the public are possible, if, as a member agency, one is not bound by the United Way's fundraising restrictions. Other sources are organizations that raise funds for charitable purposes. Fraternities and sororities often "adopt" an agency and engage in a number of small fundraising activities. A membership drive may yield substantial community support, and memorial funds may be established.

One source of revenue too few agencies explore is the publication and sale of material they have developed for use in-house. Often, with minor modification, this material has utility and relevance in other communities. Examples include two brochures developed in Ithaca, "Living Through It" and "Back From the Edge." Both focus on young people and the prevention of suicide among adolescents and college students. Training manuals may be another source of revenue. Training itself may generate income; a well-designed training program can be offered to other agencies and groups on a fee-for-service basis. A speaker's bureau might develop a fee schedule for its services. An active bureau staffed by trained volunteers can also generate considerable income for an agency. It is also possible to develop after-hours coverage contracts with agencies closing at 5:00 p.m. since most crisis programs offer their services 24-hours a day (provided the strain on crisis workers is not too great, and there are sufficient instruments available to handle extra calls). Crisis workers should not be expected to put in extra hours without appropriate compensation.

As an example, diversified funding resources support the Suicide Prevention and Crisis Service of Tompkins County in Ithaca, New York. It should be noted that many funding sources require separate budget and reporting forms, and that considerable administrative time is spent in developing and responding to these. However, diversification of funding sources strengthens the agency. It is never totally dependent on the vicissitudes of the public sector, and it is protected from grave harm if political opinions shift. Ideally, citizens should be able to take for granted their crisis service, just as they expect police and fire protection in a community. If comprehensive crisis services are in place, then, when a new crisis such as the current AIDS epidemic emerges, at least the foundation is there for rapid response and refinement of existing programs to meet new needs.

Once a program is well-established, there is the possibility of building an endowment fund. The money raised for this capital fund is invested, and the interest is made available to the agency for ongoing support. At Northeastern University in Boston, the 1987 graduating class endowed the newly developing Life Crisis Institute on campus, through their class gift, with the goal of assisting students around the AIDS crisis. Endowment funds of necessity may be central in the future of human services. Again, this is a time-consuming board function.

Needs and Resources Assessment

Many communities now have central planning agencies, such as a Human Service Coalition or the planning division of the United Way. If a crisis program is in the planning stage (about a full and intensive year of planning is essential before a program begins to function), it is important NOT to repeat past work. Planners should focus on the unique efforts required by the program envisioned. On the other hand, as new needs and awareness of underserved populations surface, it is important to address them explicitly. A San Francisco community mental health service provides an example of such an effort. It responded to the needs of the gay community, which has traditionally been stigmatized rather than served by the psychiatric community (Rabin, Keefe and Burton, 1986). Other possible sources of needs assessment information are the local Department of Social Services, the County Department of Planning, the Senior Citizens Council, the Census Bureau, the local school district, and other groups with established data collection mechanisms and plans. Community questionnaires may be disseminated. It is possible that the local newspaper may become interested in helping to publicize and, perhaps, even distribute such a planning document. Information that may be of use includes:

1. Population of catchment area, including age, sex, education, socioeconomic distribution, and other demographic factors.
2. Profiles of available services—their target populations, hours of service, rate of utilization, fee structure, etc.
3. Primary community problems (e.g., substantial number of discharged mental patients, pending factory closings, and lack of victim assistance programs.)
4. Population projections.

A necessary part of the planning process further includes an assessment of the community's resources. In these days of limited funds for human services, one of the most delicate concerns is duplication of service. It is vital to ascertain what the community already has established, and to whatever extent possible, integrate the crisis program with existing services, insisting on high standards and training. In addition, what are the possibilities for designing a particular kind of program? A service dependent on trained volunteers suggests a large community or a community with some turnover in population because volunteer crisis workers tend to invest themselves heavily and then, after a period of time, move on. A service designed to be operated by mental health professionals will obviously be more costly. Where will this money come from? What is the availability of emergency service at the local hospital or the local mental health center? Is there a shelter for victims of domestic violence?

Any planning process needs to take into consideration the particular context of the program's location. We have already mentioned this with regard to training and the nature of the problems workers are likely to confront. But context also plays a vital role in setting up programs. For example, the ethnic and racial composition of the community is a crucial planning factor. Will more than one language be important to the functioning of the agency? If the catchment area includes for example, a substantial Mexican-American population, it will be crucial to provide service in both English and Spanish. (It should be noted that Suicide Action Montreal, Inc., located in Montreal, makes every effort to have both Anglo and French speaking workers on duty at all times.) In general, the staffing pattern should replicate the community at large.

Similarly, the economic distribution of the population to be served should be considered in the planning process. Where people struggle with survival issues, adequate food and affordable shelter, the crisis program will confront harsh realities in trying to assist clients to obtain these essentials. While it is important not to assume the absence of problems with serious substance abuse, domestic violence, rape, and other traumatic events in middle or upper middle class catchment areas, it is true that police protection is often better in wealthier neighborhoods (inhabitants with money to pay for a motel in the event of a fire, adequate insurance coverage, etc.).

No crisis program can exist effectively in a vacuum. Most communities already have basic services such as emergency transportation and inpatient hospitalization. Coordination of new services with existing ones provides an efficient, effective method for helping people in crisis. Agreements should be carefully drawn up between those agencies most essential to the delivery of emergency services before any crisis intervention program opens. These would include the police, the telephone company for tracing procedures, ambulance services, immediate treatment settings if the program is not itself staffed or equipped to provide walk-in service, and emergency food and shelter providers. When a family or individual is in the midst of a crisis, the situation will only be exacerbated if the crisis worker has to start shopping around to negotiate services. This could seriously jeopardize the desired outcome of the crisis.

Since today, one or more elements of crisis service (e.g., 24-hour hotline and rescue capacity) already exist; in a typical community, future efforts should focus on:

- community examination to learn what services do and do not exist. This can be done by a survey of social and mental health agencies to determine the extent of an agency's involvement in delivering crisis services. The examination should also include citizen surveys. One rural community in Vermont found that citizens in crisis usually called on registered nurses working part-time in the community. The nurses were then enlisted, on a voluntary basis, to receive training to increase their skills as crisis workers (Marshall and Finan, 1971),

- development of crisis service elements that do not exist (e.g., 24-hour mobile capacity, outreach), and evaluation and improvement of effectiveness of those elements that already exist,
- development of a system for *maintaining* a high quality crisis service and revising it according to the changing needs of consumers. For example, as hospital emergency personnel become more sensitized to and skilled in meeting the needs of rape victims, and potential victims *know* that appropriate treatment is available there, a community may no longer need a separate rape crisis service.

When considering the development or enhancement of a community crisis service, planners must remember that crisis workers can possess all the knowledge and skills necessary for effective crisis management. Yet, if individual workers feel forced to function in isolation, without the support and help of a well-coordinated human service system, the worker's best efforts can be undermined. Individual efforts are also frustrated when administrators in specific agencies such as hospitals and mental health centers are unconvinced of crisis work's importance. Commitment to crisis service probably does not exist if it is the last area to be adequately funded and staffed, the first to be eliminated during fiscal constraint, or if workers are not provided the training, supervision, and physical environment they need to help distressed people. Communities considering the development or enhancement of crisis services should arrange at least one site visit (and possibly program consultation—see Chapter 8) to a crisis program that has met minimum standards and is certified by the AAS.

Political Considerations

While crisis workers carefully maintain clients' confidentiality, the program itself must be highly visible to be viable. This entails some political sensitivities and awareness from the staff, board, and volunteers. The service may, for example, wish to reach out to pregnant teenagers. The very issue of confidentiality may in and of itself become a politicized issue, as when a police officer calls demanding information, or a physician asks for unauthorized information about his or her patient. In addition, the service may receive demands it cannot meet; for example, a second party requests intervention in instances that might violate ethical standards. This issue is particularly sensitive when the request comes from another agency or a prominent member of the community. The best position is a reliance on clearly stated policy and an administrator who fully understands that policy and is not uncomfortable articulating it.

Politically, there are both advantages and disadvantages to running a crisis program. Service users may be reluctant to give public statements of support when the agency is threatened with a cutoff or reduction of funding. The constituency tends to be silent. An exception occurred recently in New England where a fiscal crisis was successfully resolved through the center's well-established political connections and the inclusion of consumers on its board of directors. Generally, though, families may not have the courage to name a suicide prevention center as the recipient of memorial fund donations when a death has occurred (even if the death is not a suicide). As a result, the agency needs to develop vocal support from other resources—community leaders, professionals, and other agencies. Furthermore, the agency's failures tend to be fairly public. The completed suicide is visible; the prevented suicide is almost always invisible (Miller, Coombs, Leeper, and Barton, 1984). On the other hand, crisis work is dramatic and vitally interesting, and the concern for life is one that attracts people from all parts of the political spectrum. In the hands of a skilled staff and board of directors, this interest and concern can reap substantial benefits for the agency. In addition, an agency that relies on trained volunteers has not only a broad-based group of community activists, but also an argument for financial support from those who are unable or unwilling to give their time.

Community Visibility and Public Relations

As mentioned earlier, the planning phase of the crisis program must include the careful establishment of good community relations. This means taking the time to meet with agency directors, community leaders, potential funding sources, advisors, and others important to the program's success. They will have visible as well as hidden agendas; the latter may include concerns about turf and other territorial anxieties. Professionals may feel challenged by a different approach to helping people and may distrust the use of volunteers as entry-point workers. Police may be cynical about the crisis program responding when needed, given their too frequent past experience with unresponsive mental health workers. Religious leaders may be concerned about the program's stance on right-to-life issues. Social service administrators may be concerned that crisis workers will become demanding advocates for clients who are not truly eligible for assistance.

An effective organization not only addresses these problems through the composition of its board of directors, but through a commitment to a public relations program that includes regular meetings with community groups who have any concerns about or interactions with the agency. The executive director must be prepared to respond to complaints about the program in an open and non-defensive manner, to hear the complaint fully and fairly, to bring together whenever possible the people involved, and to negotiate some mutually satisfactory resolution. In addition, efforts should be made to establish a working relationship with the press. The agency will depend on the press for publicity regarding its programs, fundraising efforts, community relations, and support during a possible funding crisis.

Finally, the crisis program must find ways to be visible in the community. Numerous strategies accomplish this—wide distribution of brochures describing agency services, cards listing the agency number (for political clout, listing other emergency numbers in the community, which reduces resistance to their distribution), articles in local papers, and radio and television interviews. The agency may persuade the telephone company to include a listing of the crisis number in the telephone directory's inside cover and in as many ways as possible and affordable (example—Crisis, Suicide Prevention, Rape Crisis, Emergency Counseling, etc.).

An effective speaker's bureau is another method of maintaining good public relations and increasing community visibility. Initially, the agency may wish to target certain groups, senior citizens, PTA's, and others. (The role of a speaker's bureau is discussed further in Chapter 8.) It is highly likely that, if the speakers are effective, requests will soon exceed the bureau's capacity to respond. It is always useful to bring agency material to speaking engagements, both for recruiting volunteers and for informing potential clients of the range of agency services. Agency staff should also join community planning committees, sit on relevant boards, and become as integrated in the community as possible. It is no more appropriate for an agency director and some of the other staff to be strictly office-based than it is for a crisis program to offer its services only in the office from 9 to 5. In general, the public relations program will be more effective if coordinated by a person with marketing skills and sufficient time than if it is conducted on a piecemeal basis by persons unconvinced of the importance of this vital agency function.

References

Marshall, C., and J. L. Finan. 1971. "The indigenous nurse as a crisis counselor." *Bulletin of Suicidology,* Washington, D.C.: National Institute of Mental Health.

Miller, H. L., D. W. Coombs, J. D. Leeper, and S. N. Barton. 1984. "An analysis of the effects of suicide prevention facilities on suicide rates in the United States." *American Journal of Public Health,* 74(4):340–343.

Rabin, J., K. Keefe, and M. Burton. 1986. "Enhancing services for sexual-minority clients: A community mental health approach." *Social Work,* July–August:294–298.

6

Crisis Programs: Service Elements and Organizational Structure

Introduction* ▬▬▬▬▬▬▬▬▬▬▬▬▬▬▬▬▬▬▬▬

This book assumes that every community assures its members in crisis that help is available *when* they need it and *where* it will do the most good—in their real-life, natural community setting. As noted earlier, the existence of a crisis service in a community should be as routine as the presence of police and fire protection, postal service, and schools.

Much has been written concerning various crises and what to do about them. Authors have described programs that fit specific communities, a large metropolitan area, a small town, or an isolated rural area. Much less has been written about the structures crisis workers function in and the organizational factors that influence their work with people in crisis. But, how do these factors all *come together* in a practical and workable design? What are the principles and guidelines that should characterize all crisis programs regardless of individual differences specific to certain settings?

Crisis specialists, suicidologists, victim advocates, government agencies (e.g., the NIMH in the United States), state departments of mental health, the Joint Commission on Accreditation of Hospitals (JCAH-Community Mental Health division), and the American Association of Suicidology have set guidelines for the organization and delivery of comprehensive crisis services. These guidelines provide practical assistance to boards of directors and program administrators who wish to implement a service and/or evaluate and refine existing crisis services. A comprehensive crisis service should include several basic elements, regardless of organizational model. These service elements are

1. Twenty-four hour telephone service.
2. Face-to-face crisis service—walk-in access to crisis centers in local neighborhoods and 24-hour crisis outreach to homes and other community settings.
3. Emergency medical/psychiatric service—emergency assessment of suicide or other risk to life, availability of emergency medication (preferably from a physician with thorough knowledge of psychotropic drugs), and linkage to a psychiatric inpatient service.
4. Linkage network with established community emergency services —

* Originally published in *People in Crisis*, 1st ed. (Menlo Park, CA: Addison-Wesley, 1978). Reprinted with permission of publisher.

police and rescue squads, Traveler's Aid, and other community resources. The network should include standing agreements and a procedure for convening emergency planning conferences when necessary to resolve a crisis constructively (Hansell, 1976; Hoff, 1984a, Ch. 5; Polak, 1971; Garrison, 1974).

It is unnecessary and impossible in most communities to administer these services through a single agency. The important requirement is coordination and assurance that one element of service does *not* operate in isolation from the others.

Telephone Service

Twenty-four hour telephone emergency service has had a major impact on launching the suicide prevention and crisis intervention movement in the United States (Farberow and Shneidman, 1961) and Great Britain (The Samaritans). Telephone services, the backbone of the crisis movement, are operated predominantly by lay volunteers with consultation and supervision from professional crisis workers. The crisis telephone service comprises, in fact, the major entry point for many to the formal mental health system.

Important as the telephone service is, however, it is not adequate by itself. Volunteer telephone counselors must be able to put a caller in touch with a face-to-face counselor or mobilize an outreach team when needed. Indeed, for some groups—the elderly and Native Americans in the United States and other isolated people living in rural outposts worldwide—telephones are often not accessible or in good enough working order to be useful during a crisis. Another limitation of 24-hour telephone service, if not linked with other elements of service, is that people at greatest risk are the least likely to use this service. If a telephone service is run largely to meet the needs of a white middle class population, the service will not help many high risk groups. Homeless persons in the United States, two-thirds of whom are discharged mental patients, are a current example of such a high risk group with little or no inclination or financial ability to use telephones during periods of crisis. Similar circumstances exist among the poor in many developing countries. Nevertheless, the telephone service has been expanded in many communities to include services to special groups (Berlatsky, 1982). Some communities now have teen hotlines, drug hotlines, parents-in-crisis, rape crisis lines, services for battered women, the hearing impaired, and victims of AIDS.

Face-To-Face Service: Walk-in ▬▬▬▬▬▬▬ and Outreach

In this book, face-to-face crisis service refers to the work of mental health crisis clinics (or centers) designed specifically to offer assistance to distressed people by specially trained crisis counselors. The term does not imply, however, that face-to-face crisis services exist *only* in such agencies. For example, medical and nursing personnel in hospital emergency settings, police officers, and other community caretakers such as victim advocates routinely do face-to-face crisis work. But as discussed in earlier chapters, programs preparing such workers do not usually include more than a smattering of content to prepare them for confident and skilled functioning with people in crisis. However, community and mainstream health care workers can provide this kind of face-to-face crisis assistance when trained according to national standards.

Face-to-face crisis service can be offered as an adjunct to a 24-hour telephone service, as an integral part of a community mental health center, or as a facet of a hospital-based emergency mental health service. SPCS, Inc. of Ithaca, New York illustrates the first context. The Central New Hampshire Community Mental Health Center in Concord represents the second. The Boston City Hospital emergency service represents the third. People can "walk in" to such centers or be referred by others. These centers are the chief back-up service for teachers, police, nurses, physicians, and pastoral workers, all the people who most often have the *first* face-to-face contact with people in crisis.

Face-to-face crisis service should be organized for mobile capacity. If a person or family in crisis is unable, for whatever reason, to come to a crisis center, experienced counselors must be ready and able to go as necessary to the home or other community setting to intervene in acute crisis situations. Over the past couple of decades, the experience of crisis centers and specialists reveals that crisis outreach work, when carefully planned and supervised, is not necessary very often. However, when mobile capacity *is* called for and is not available, the consequences can be drastic in terms of time spent later on reconstructive work and, sometimes, in terms of lost lives. Crisis outreach work is indicated in the following circumstances:

1. When a crisis situation cannot be adequately assessed by telephone.

For example, the caller is being interrupted by an extremely upset family member, making telephone assessment impossible.

2. When the police or rescue squad are inappropriate, refused by the caller, or unavailable. For example, the following tragedy occurred in one community that had no crisis outreach service.

> A mentally disturbed man was brought to a hospital emergency room by two police officers for psychiatric examination. On the way out of the car, the man grabbed one of the officers' gun and shot him. The other officer in turn shot the patient. The patient died instantly and the police officer died a few hours later. Although this man had a history of mental disturbance, he carried no lethal weapons at the time of the police investigation. If crisis outreach workers had been available to this family, they might have prevented two unnecessary deaths.

3. When immediate assistance is needed to avoid acute family disruption and possible forced removal of a person from the home.

4. When there is acute danger of suicide and the person cannot or will not come to a clinic or hospital for help. This implies thorough assessment according to established criteria.

5. When there is possible danger of violence toward others. By telephone, the crisis counselor should determine if lethal weapons are involved. If so, the case should be handled collaboratively with the police. This implies that prior working relationships with the police have been developed to avoid crisis escalation by police presence. Police officers do not appreciate being called to assist in life-threatening crisis situations and then being advised by mental health professionals on how to conduct themselves. If crisis workers have suggestions for police officers about handling such cases, they should be made in the context of in-service training or consultation programs *prior* to, *not during* acute crisis situations. At no time are mental health crisis workers expected to place themselves in situations that are openly dangerous to their own lives.

People doing specialized crisis work in outreach situations should be highly skilled in assessing risk for suicide and violence toward others and working with police and other emergency services (Hatton and Valente, 1984; Hoff, 1984a, Chapters 6 and 8). They should also be capable of mobilizing emergency housing facilities and making hospitalization arrangements (including involuntary commitment) when necessary. They also serve as consultants and supporters to frontline crisis workers such as nurses, physicians, police, rescue workers, and teachers (Briar, 1985). A trained group of crisis workers capable of such community outreach work can prevent many possible destructive outcomes of crisis. At *no time* should a crisis worker be expected to staff a walk-in crisis center alone or make crisis outreach visits alone. Any staff member requested to do so, for whatever reason (e.g., staffing or funding shortage), should vigorously refuse. While most distressed people are not dangerous, inattention to this precaution can result in loss of life or physical and psychological injury.

Emergency Medical/Psychiatric Service

The initial step of this service element is carried out by specialized crisis workers, rescue squads, volunteer fire departments, and the police. Hospital emergency departments and emergency services of community mental health centers also play a large role in the complete delivery of this service element. An effective crisis service must have reliable working relationships with psychiatric, medical, and hospital establishments. Physicians, preferably psychiatrists, should be available as part of the team, at least as consultants, when medication and hospitalization are needed. Community crisis centers and hospital emergency departments should have established agreements with crisis hostels as an alternative to psychiatric hospitalization whenever it is impossible to maintain a person in crisis in his or her natural community (Polak and Kirby, 1976). In those instances when medication and psychiatric hospitalization are indicated, neither should be delayed because of poor working relationships with the medical community.

Community Linkage Network

Effective and comprehensive crisis work in a community includes establishing clear working agreements and referral procedures with all agencies involved in crisis work. In practice, this means that referral procedures and telephone numbers should be available to all involved agencies. Also, in hospital emergency departments and physicians' offices, information cards describing local crisis counseling services and phone numbers should be made available to clients. This is especially important for those who have made suicide attempts or have been victimized by crime and still receive *only* medical treatment in some general hospitals. Police might also distribute such information.

A formal written agreement is certainly not a guarantee against interagency communication problems. However, such agreements provide a context for workers to resolve some of the problems and misunderstandings that occur in crisis work. The larger the community, the more important formal agreements become. Bureaucratic red tape is less complicated in smaller communities. Also, working relationships in smaller communities are usually more closely knit, thereby preventing the "systems" problems prevalent in metropolitan communities.

A "systems" problem occurs when the network of community agencies does not work together in a cohesive manner to help people in crisis. Formal agreements, which include a review process, can reduce this hazard to effective crisis work.

Organization Models

The essential elements of a comprehensive crisis service can and do exist in a variety of models. Richard McGee (1974) describes several models in *Crisis Intervention in the Community*. Organizational models can be distinguished in several respects —the origin of the program (indigenous community effort or government mandate), the comprehensiveness of service (single or multi-service), the type of funding supporting the service (public, private, or mixed), and the authority structure or manner in which decisions are made and accountability rendered (hierarchical, consensus, or mixed).

Crisis service models in the United States

Examples of different models in the United States include:

1. A crisis center with its own policy board to provide all elements of service within its own program. This type of model often originates through the volunteer efforts of mental health associations, ministerial associations, or other voluntary citizen groups. This and the following model grew from the work of Edwin Shneidman, Norman Farberow, and colleagues at the Los Angeles Suicide Prevention Center over three decades ago (1957, 1961).

2. A 24-hour telephone service relies on agreements with various

private and public agencies to provide face-to-face service, including walk-in and outreach.

3. A community mental health program provides walk-in and outreach services. It has its own or relies on another local hotline for 24-hour telephone coverage. This model evolved from the federal mental health legislation of the early 1960s mandating the delivery of emergency mental health services as a part of all community mental health programs.

4. A public health hospital or detention center on a Native American reservation or other rural community relies on the police and community health workers for word-of-mouth contacts with distressed people, since few of the residents have phones (Shore, Bopp, Waller, and Dawes, 1972).

5. A public or private general hospital with an emergency department that includes on-site crisis specialists, psychiatric consultants, and outreach service organized as a discrete element of the hospital emergency service.

Variations of these models may exist on college or university campuses and other institutions (e.g., the armed services) that provide health services for their constituencies.

International models

The best known international model of a crisis service is The Samaritans. This organization began in the British Isles in 1953 when the Reverend Chad Varah started a counseling service in his London church for despairing and suicidal people. His service became widely known and was used by a large number of people. Friendly volunteers offered to help by chatting or having a cup of tea with clients waiting to see Reverend Varah. To his surprise, some people no longer needed his counseling after they had been informally helped by volunteers. Thus a disciplined lay organization, The Samaritans, for befriending troubled and suicidal people was born. In 1963, Samaritans Incorporated, a national association, was formed to protect the name and basic principles of The Samaritans. Today, there are hundreds of branches in Great Britain and on every continent.

The Samaritans are similar to many United States' crisis centers in their independence from the official helping bureaucracy that many people fear and suspect will have them "put away" in hospitals if they seek help. In general, these alternative models were fueled by the student and civil rights protests of the 1960s that objected to traditional hierarchical structures interferring with the humane delivery of service to people in crisis. Today, these non-hierarchical models are represented by women in crisis services that grew from the women's movement and women's health movement. For battered women in life-threatening situations, Great Britain was also the site for a grassroots movement that has spread to many countries and continents. While some services for victimized women, including victimization by rape, operate along traditional hierarchical lines of authority, many espouse a consensus model for the sharing of power and decision making in egalitarian fashion. The major strength of such models is the sense of inclusion all workers feel. Their major weakness is the inefficiency that can result from the time-consuming process required for workers' maximum participation. Increasingly, organizations are combining elements of both traditional and consensus authority structures as an avenue for increasing workers' participation without sacrificing efficiency.

More and more today, specialized services are being incorporated into mainstream health services with more widespread acceptance of the need for public support (including crisis intervention) for all victims of crime or disadvantaged groups. On the other hand, there is concern among some of these grassroots movements, especially for women, about co-optation and subsequent loss of attention to the political aspects of victimization rooted in social inequality and the recent backlash against civil rights gains (Schechter, 1982; Withorn, 1980; Hoff, 1984b).

Another international model is the International Federation of Telephone Emergency Services (IFOTES). This group is particularly present on the European continent. Member agencies of IFOTES perform a very valuable service for distressed people, although they are limited to assisting people on the telephone. As with other telephone programs, it is important to establish formal linkages with agencies offering face-to-face services.

Generally the Samaritans, the battered women's shelter movement, and similar alternative services for distressed people illustrate a basic principle of the crisis movement: One need not be a professional with years of training to help people who are despaired, suicidal, or threatened by violence. The work of Samaritan volunteers and thousands like them apparently makes a life and death difference to significant numbers of people world-wide.

Community-wide Coordination of ▬▬▬▬▬▬▬
Crisis Services

Each community should develop a model and authority structure that suits its unique circumstances. Regardless of the model, however, a crisis service should include these essential characteristics:

1. Various caretakers, such as police and rescue workers, health, and mental health workers, *coordinate* their efforts to offer their services to people in crisis (or develop them, if currently not available).

2. Local citizens/consumers have a voice in developing the service.

3. Service is relevant, i.e., tailored to local needs, available, visible, and accessible to the people it serves.

4. Consumers have a voice in monitoring the delivery of crisis services. They should be strongly represented on a board of directors or advisory committees. When citizens know that their opinion is valued, they invariably offer rich suggestions for service development that is relevant to their needs.

5. Leaders in human service agencies assume responsibility for assuring a coordinated, effective delivery of crisis service.

References

Berlatsky, T. 1982. "The help line: An agency response to a community crisis." *Social Casework*, April:241–243.

Briar, K. H. 1985. "Emergency calls to police: Implications for social work intervention." *Social Service Review*, December:593 – 603.

Farberow, N. L., and E. S. Shneidman, eds. 1961. *The cry for help*. New York: McGraw-Hill.

Garrison, J. 1974. "Network techniques: Case studies in the screening-linking-planning conference method." *Family process*, 13:337–353.

Hansell, N. 1976. *The person in distress*. New York: Human Sciences Press.

Hatton, C., S. Valente, and A. Rink. 1984. *Suicide: Assessment and intervention*. 2nd ed. New York: Appleton-Century-Crofts.

Hoff, L. A. 1984a. *People in crisis: Understanding and helping*. Menlo Park: Addison-Wesley.

Hoff, L. A. 1984b. *Violence against women: A social-cultural network analysis*. Ph.D. dissertation. Boston: Boston University.

McGee, R. K. 1974. *Crisis intervention in the community*. Baltimore: University Park Press.

Polak, P. R. 1971. "Social systems intervention." *Archives of General Psychiatry*, 25:110–117.

Polak, P. R., and M. W. Kirby. 1976. "A model to replace psychiatric hospitalization." *Journal of Nervous and Mental Disease*, 162:13 –22.

Schechter, S. 1982. *Women and male violence*. Boston: South End Press.

Shneidman, E. S., and N. L. Farberow, eds. 1957. *Clues to suicide*. New York: McGraw-Hill.

Shore, J. H., J. F. Bopp, T. R. Waller, and J. W. Dawes. 1972. "A suicide prevention center on an Indian reservation." *American Journal of Psychiatry*, 128:1086–91.

Withorn, A. 1980. "Helping ourselves." *Radial America*, 14:25 –39.

7

Crisis Programs: Management and Evaluation

Staff Screening and Selection ████████████████████

The success of a crisis service depends heavily on the selection of appropriate staff. The extensive experience of crisis trainers and supervisors clearly reveals that not everyone is suited to do crisis work. There are many rewards, continuous excitement, and challenges in the crisis arena; but, there is also considerable stress and some danger. These factors must be kept in mind in the recruitment, training, and supervision of crisis workers. A person whose tolerance for stress is low and attitude is unsuitable, or who feels forced into an unwanted assignment will be part of the problem rather than the solution in acute crisis situations.

On the other hand, if staff members are appropriately selected, trained, supervised, and provided on-going support, there will be no shortage of people willing and able to do the job. Therefore, the job should not be forced on those who do not want it. Recognition of this staff screening principle will eliminate many problems stemming from staff ineffectiveness or poor attitudes. It will also save many dollars in training time, orientations due to less staff turnover, and perhaps even losses from lawsuits by injured clients. At best, it is shortsighted to expect ill-suited or unwilling people to do crisis work. At worst, the lack of staff screening can result in inadequate crisis service for those entitled to it, all citizens of a community.

Staffing Patterns* ████████████████████████████████

Staffing should be determined by the kind and extent of service the agency offers. People doing crisis work need the support of a clearly defined staffing arrangement. Crisis workers must know who their teammates are and whom to call for consultation or other assistance. Crisis counselors and mental health professionals doing crisis work must possess an attitude of flexibility about their work hours. Workers responsible for consultation and outreach must be willing to be "on call." However, a crisis worker should not be expected to be on call more than one or two nights a week, the ideal being once every 10 to 14 days, depending on staff size and volume of service.

* Originally printed in *People in Crisis*, 1st ed. (Menlo Park, CA: Addison-Wesley, 1978). Reprinted with permission of publisher.

Mechanical devices such as a beeper system should be part of any well run crisis service. This increases the reliability of the call system and frees workers from remaining beside a phone during the entire call period. It also reduces the prospect of staff burnout from being on call.

Staffing arrangements must also include provision for the staff to take time off when they have worked into the evening and night hours on crisis outreach calls. This is unnecessary in agencies that are sufficiently budgeted to pay staff for call-time, even when no calls are made. However, many crisis agencies do not have the budget for such reimbursement. General hospitals that do not already have mental health specialists with crisis expertise routinely available to emergency department staff should make every effort to develop such a program (Boston City Hospital has had a program like this for years). Emergency personnel who do not have this assistance will be less able to act as crisis managers in hospital emergency settings.

Team Relationships in Crisis Work ▬▬▬▬▬▬▬▬

Team relationships are important in carrying out any human service function. In crisis work, team relationships are critical. The effective use of social network techniques in crisis intervention demands that we relate with clarity and effectiveness to other people who are helping. Social network techniques demand a minimum of two people for constructive outcomes. In high risk suicidal or homicidal situations in the home or elsewhere, the presence of *at least two team members* is essential as a resource and for safety.

When distressed people come to an agency for help, they should be informed that the entire agency team is available to them. The emergency telephone number of the agency, never the counselor's home number, should be given to the person. Giving someone a personal telephone number for emergencies implies that the counselor will be available for all possible emergencies. If a distressed person calls and the counselor is not there, a serious credibility problem can result. Counselors cannot and should not attempt to provide twenty-four hour crisis service single-handedly. To do so may result in what has been called the "burn-out syndrome." That is, after six months or so, the exhausted and overspent counselor gives up and might abandon crisis work altogether. However, people in crisis do need 24-hour service available. This can only be provided by an agency or community plan designed for such continuous service. Twenty-four hour emergency coverage demands that all agency staff members collaborate as a team.

Teamwork is also vital for offering encouragement to partners while working with clients. Strain is inevitable when dealing regularly with life and death matters as well as other traumatic life events. For example, if a person who is receiving counseling commits suicide, the counselor is one of the survivors who needs someone to talk with about the traumatic experience. *Counselors are people too.* Their supply of energy is not inexhaustible. One of their sources of "refueling" for more crisis work is the support and active cooperation of fellow team members.

Role of Volunteers

In spite of the fact that volunteers are the backbone of various crisis sevices (suicide prevention, drug hotlines, battered women's shelters, rape hotlines), they are sometimes treated like second-class citizens. For example, some volunteer telephone counselors are not allowed to counsel clients face-to-face. Allegedly, the telephone counselor is not sufficiently skilled for this task. This practice is ironic on several counts:

1. It implies that a caller in crisis is in worse shape *after* the telephone intervention than before, when the opposite is usually true. If people in crisis use the telephone at all, they usually use it at the peak of their distress.

2. Helping a person in crisis by telephone intervention often requires *more* skill than counseling on a face-to-face basis. The telephone counselor relies on verbal and voice cues only and has less opportunity to "control" the counseling situation ("control" here is used in the sense of directing the counseling interaction). The caller can always hang up, leaving the counselor very frustrated. In contrast, face-to-face counseling allows for many more situational supports.

3. Over the phone or face-to-face, crisis intervention is crisis intervention. The telephone is one of the many devices available to a crisis worker. If a volunteer has mastered the basics of crisis management, he or she should be able to help a person in crisis either over the telephone *or* face-to-face. Volunteers who are trained to practice crisis intervention according to only one mode, the telephone, are only partially trained. If a crisis volunteer is trained to help people

express feelings and understand their crisis situation, to assess risk to life, and to develop and implement a plan for crisis resolution, then that person can practice the same techniques face-to-face.

Perhaps one reason for not allowing telephone counselors to work with clients face-to-face is that in some settings such work is really psychotherapy, not crisis intervention. Most crisis workers are not trained to do psychotherapy, and some professional psychotherapists are not trained to do crisis intervention. Optimally, helpers should do only what they are trained to do, but not be prevented from doing it fully.

All of us do formal or informal crisis intervention in our everyday lives. People who formally help other people in crisis are referred to as "crisis workers" or "crisis counselors." No distinction should be made between those who do crisis work as volunteers and those who work for financial remuneration. Volunteer crisis workers are the thousands of women and men who provide approximately 85% of the staff of 24-hour telephone crisis services throughout many countries. Some of these same volunteers do outreach work and face-to-face counseling with distressed people. These crisis workers are often referred to as the "real professionals" in the crisis field (McGee and Jennings, 1973).

Those who volunteer their time as crisis workers do so because of their dedication and interest in this work as their chosen way of helping others. Most volunteers also claim that the experience promotes personal growth. This often depends on the nature of team relationships and the quality of supervision they receive. Volunteer crisis workers earn their living as accountants, teachers, writers, psychologists, homemakers, nurses, secretaries, etc. They work several hours weekly or monthly as crisis service volunteers. They are not paid and do not rely on the work as a means of supporting themselves. "Paid" crisis workers may be full-time crisis specialists and should also include nurses, physicians, police, and rescue workers constantly in contact with people in crisis.

Another group of crisis workers are volunteer or paid fire fighters and rescue workers. Their vital work in the community is often taken for granted. Although their immediate concern is to put out fires and provide physical support before the person is brought to a hospital, such workers are not generally included in the development of a community's comprehensive crisis services. Yet, fire fighters and rescue workers are always called in cases of suicide attempts. They are also left with the job of consoling the survivors of accidents or the relatives of a heart attack victim. Such situations certainly require crisis intervention skills. These volunteers should not be neglected as part of the total community "staff " of crisis workers. In addition, they may themselves need assistance when they have worked with a particularly difficult situation, such as an accident or abuse resulting in the death of a child. An excellent resource for volunteer management issues is Volunteer—The National Center, 1111 North 19th St., Suite 5000, Arlington, VA 22209.

Qualifications of Clinical Supervisors

Although some people seem to have innate abilities as leaders, there are some identifiable qualifications and skills that a supervisor needs. A good supervisor thinks of supervisees as persons, not just another "spoke in the wheel" of the agency. This includes an attitude of respect and concern and an appreciation of the person's basic needs and growth goals. An effective supervisor also values and respects her or his own role as supervisor. Additionally, the supervisor should possess managerial competence in several areas:

1. Knowledge and skill in the area to supervise or consult (in this case, crisis management).
2. Ability to share these skills with another in a non-threatening way. *Example:* "What do you think about trying . . .?" (Supervisor suggests a well-established approach to a problem presented by supervisee.)
3. Capable of assessing a worker's skills and needs. *Example:* Supervisor and supervisee meet to explore problem areas the worker needs help in.
4. Ability to involve the worker in the supervisory process. *Example:* (Supervisor to worker) "Considering your experience in working with this person, what do you think about the approach we've discussed?"
5. Ability to offer recognition and support when indicated. *Example:* "John, from what you've described, I think you did a terrific job helping. . . ."
6. Capable of providing clear and concrete direction when indicated. *Example:* "I suggest you call the rescue squad immediately."

Those who are supervised or need consultation should also possess certain attitudes in order to obtain the greatest benefit from the supervisory process:

1. Self-confidence regarding one's abilities, needs, and potential for growth.
2. An attitude of openness toward learning, the supervisor, and the supervisory process.
3. Acceptance of the agency's goals.
4. Acceptance of one's role in the agency once appropriately defined in relation to one's skills and experience. Some workers are in trouble because of a very unrealistic concept of themselves and the skills they possess.

Administrative structures that clearly spell out authority and consultative roles can also eliminate many problems. Authority roles are either ascribed or achieved. An ascribed authority role is acquired by a legitimate administrative appointment. Achieved authority is acquired by virtue of experience, wisdom, and skill in one's field which has earned respect. Some people, unfortunately, function with *responsibility* to supervise but possess neither ascribed nor achieved authority. Such a situation is problematic and unproductive for both the supervisor and the worker. People supervised in this kind of relationship have a hard time accepting the directions and suggestions of the supervisor. Any supervisors who find themselves in this untenable position should take steps to have it remedied. The supervisory responsibility can either be refused or the authority that should accompany the function can be insisted on.

Differentiating Supervision from Related Functions

One of the frequent problems encountered in the supervisory process is the failure to distinguish sharply between supervision, consultation, teaching, training, counseling/therapy, crisis intervention, and friendship. For example, a supervisor relying on her or his relationships with supervisees for friendship may experience difficulty in shifting back and forth in roles. Friendship with a supervisee is not unquestionable, but, the roles must be distinguished. Supervisors assure that a particular job, in this case, crisis work, is done in a fashion worthy of the people served. As a bonus, friendship may emerge in the process. However, some supervisory functions can engender dislike or even hostility, e.g., corrective action for the volunteer or paid worker consistently late or absent from scheduled work without notice.

Another problem that can interfere in the supervisory function is a supervisor's tendency to play "therapist" with a worker who either has or is *perceived* to have personal problems. Also, workers with personal problems sometimes try to use the supervisor as a therapist. This is best handled by focusing on the worker's actual performance. If and when personal problems interfere with job performance, the supervisor should point this out to the worker. Outside counseling sources may be recommended. Being attentive and supportive to a personally distressed worker and doing crisis intervention for that person is appropriate and recommended practice. "Therapizing" is not. There is an art to being accessible or inaccessible and knowing when and how to apply either way of helping another.

Muriel James in *The OK Boss,* transactional analysis applied to the "bossing" role, provides many useful suggestions to "bosses" for evaluating and improving their bossing style. Table 7.1 is also offered as an aid to clarify the sometimes blurred roles between supervision, consultation, therapy, friendship, etc. Continuing education programs on supervision and consultation are valuable means of elaborating on these human interaction processes in the crisis field.

Maintaining A Program ▬▬▬▬▬▬▬▬▬▬▬▬▬▬

Addressing staff burnout ▬▬▬▬▬▬▬▬▬▬▬▬

It is imperative to provide as supportive a working climate as possible for people engaged in any high stress work. Crisis work frequently involves long hours and evening work taking one away from home and family. Decisions can involve life safety. Arranging time for paperwork and meetings is difficult because the worker must be prepared for interruptions at any moment. Clients are not always cooperative and pleasant, especially if it is necessary to provide trace and rescue services. And, the demand often exceeds the worker's capacity to respond (Walfish, 1983).

Furthermore, for people situated only at the entry point, like telephone crisis counselors, there is frequently no sure way to know the outcome of a crisis situation if the call is prematurely terminated,

Table 7.1

Interactional process	Objective	Person directed toward	Methods or techniques	Relationship
Supervision: clinical and administrative	To assure quality control and agency accountability for service to clients. Survival of the agency.	Staff members (paid and volunteer).	Goal and problem assessment and clarification. Demonstration and/or role modeling. Concrete direction. Constructive criticism. Offer of recognition and support.	Line (authority).
Consultation	To offer necessary assistance in the delivery of crisis and mental health services.	Staff member or other agency staff member.	Problem and goal clarification. Suggestions and recommendations.	Staff (non-authority): may be contractual.
Teaching	To convey knowledge in a defined subject area.	Student in a formal educational program.	Lecture-discussion. Demonstration/role-playing. Reading. Audio-Visual methods. Special assignments and projects.	Contractual between student and teacher concerning subject areas only.
Training	To convey knowledge, skills, and attitudes specific to a defined functional task (e.g., crisis management).	Staff member assigned to perform a specific job function (e.g., Crisis Worker).	Lecture-discussion. Demonstration/role-playing. Reading. Audio-Visual methods. Special assignments and projects. Role modeling.	Contractual between trainee and trainer concerning training module only.
Counseling/therapy	To assist another individual/family to resolve personal or other life problems.	Client	As indicated by needs of client e.g., individual, group, marital or family therapy/counseling.	Contractual between client and counselor/agency.
Crisis intervention	To help people in crisis resolve their crisis constructively.	Anyone in crisis.	Crisis management on individual, family, or group basis. Decision counseling.	Contractual between crisis worker and person in crisis.
Friendship	To provide personal needs for support, intimacy, and social attachments.	Anyone	Communications, sharing of feelings, and commonly enjoyed activities, stress, pain, joy, sorrow, etc.	Reciprocal, mutual attachment or intimacy.

Supervision: Differentiations from Related Functions

97

or if the caller refuses to provide identifying information that makes follow-up possible. The worker is left with uncertainties about his or her performance and the results of a contact. Crisis workers may rush to the obituary page of the local newspaper, especially if they have been working with a client whose safety is of great concern. Such workers will probably need assistance around issues of responsibility, detachment, etc.

For paid staff, salaries, as in most human service agency work, are often low. Unfortunately, crisis work seldom has high status in the community, and upward mobility may be limited unless the worker has an opportunity to gain some administrative skills. Also, human service organizations tend to offer the greatest financial incentive to those in managerial roles, while neglecting those who consistently provide excellent clinical service.

Agencies must respond to the threat of staff burnout at two levels, preventively and reactively. The agency must provide sufficient compensatory time (the executive director must monitor the staff to ensure that they take it) for extra hours worked. While pay scales are relatively low, the board of directors should provide as attractive a benefits package as possible, including paid holidays and adequate vacation and sick leave. Personal days off may be included as part of the sick-leave package; these should be considered "mental health" days, requiring no justification. Few crisis workers abuse any privileges; most bring to their work a high level of idealism and commitment. The agency is protecting them, and itself, against their burnout. Furthermore, it may be possible to rotate crisis workers so that they are on for a period of time, then, switched to other activities to obtain relief from pressure.

The director, coordinator of volunteers, or whoever is in the appropriate position must be sensitive to the experience of the worker. Some situations elicit particularly strong feelings, like working with a child victim of sexual abuse. The door of this supportive person must remain open to the worker and a clear message of availability and accessibility be given. Open communication is as necessary to the functioning of the crisis program as it is to the person in crisis. Adequate consultation for the worker is essential. In fact, it is not unlike the message the agency wishes to convey to the public. The agency must itself provide or arrange to have available, needed professional consultation on any difficult issue that the worker cannot handle alone. Elisabeth Kubler-Ross has written about the need grieving people have for a "screaming room;" most crisis workers could benefit from a safe place to discharge their tensions and, at times, their anger. Staff meetings should be scheduled on a regular basis, and a periodic staff retreat is a useful tool for long-range planning and problem-solving. This is best conducted out of the office, away from telephones, and other interruptions. Staff cohesiveness and support are crucial to the prevention of burnout.

The executive director can also prevent burnout by being actively responsive to complaints the worker may have. If, for example, the worker assesses a client as highly suicidal and persuades the client to go to the local psychiatric emergency room where a cursory assessment is made without consulting the worker, and the client is not admitted, the director must be prepared to make contact with the emergency room, to obtain needed information about the experience, and when appropriate, to advocate for the staff member. There is considerably less burnout among staff who experience their director, and at a greater distance, their board of directors as supportive. In-service training is another method for combatting burnout. It provides a sense that the agency cares enough about its staff to invest time and money in continued learning. It also strengthens the capacity of workers to deal with stressful situations.

Special issues: Chronicity

Anyone who has ever attended a conference of crisis center staff has probably noted the substantial number of papers, discussion sessions, and general conversations about the problem of chronicity. Crisis centers appropriately do not see themselves in the business of maintaining lonely people through long chats on the telephone or working for years and years with clients who cycle in and out of institutional care. Furthermore, there are real concerns about people who get addicted to the crisis service, as others do to call-in radio shows.

From our perspective, there are two major issues that need to be considered with regard to chronicity, the impact on the client and the impact on the staff. Clients who demand repeat service over an extended period of time are probably not truly appropriate for a crisis service. On the other hand, there are few agencies providing the kind of ongoing support available through a 24-hour service and staffed by enough different crisis workers so that the burnout factor on an individual worker is minimized. This is particularly true of telephone crisis services that tend to attract an ongoing clientele; they are then defined as a problem to the agency. The problem of chronicity is most troublesome when telephone services are not effectively integrated with face-to-face counseling programs and other community services.

For some clients, repeated contact with the crisis service may be counterproductive. They may use the service to defuse rising tensions, rather than make the commitment to psychotherapy, which may be needed to change long-standing behavior patterns. Or they may use the service to countervene the work they are doing in therapy, and attempt to pit therapist and crisis service against each other. In addition, they may be in contact with numerous other helping agencies, thoroughly confusing themselves by participating in too many plans and programs. Records reveal that numerous suicidal clients are already in therapy making contact with the crisis service to discuss their suicidal feelings. When asked if the therapist is aware of their self-destructive mood, the response too often is "Oh no, I couldn't tell my therapist about that." It is difficult to know if the therapist has conveyed a subtle message that it is not okay for the client to discuss suicide, or if the client is being either untruthful or unnecessarily timid. In either case, it is the responsibility of the worker to assess risk and attempt to open communication between client and therapist.

In addition, there is a subtle message a crisis service can promote if not careful. When a client is in crisis, everything stops to provide support and immediate access to service. Family members may be encouraged to help the individual through the crisis period. Employers may be advised to back off for a period of time. And, in general, the support structure may be strengthened. But, without effective crisis management, which includes post-crisis planning, it is entirely possible that once the danger is past, the support may be withdrawn and the individual is left with the message that only when in acute trouble can he or she truly get needs met.

Frequently, chronicity is a problem for people diagnosed as having borderline personality disorders, minimal interpersonal skills, or marginal ability to cope with the daily stresses of life (Kotkov, 1983). Some centers refuse repeated contact with these clients, denying them access to the crisis line; others set firm limits; still others accept all calls from all callers. One of the most useful directions one can take with a repeat client is to develop a clear action plan as early as possible. Another strategy, especially for a multi-service user, is to call a case conference, with the client's cooperation and participation. All of the helpers in the individual's network should be invited. A useful question for the convener to ask is what the client thinks he or she needs from each agency represented, and then ask the agency to respond to the expressed need. A plan for appropriate use of services can be developed with the client at the center as a willing participant. An agreement can be drawn up and distributed. This may alleviate the pitting of one agency against another, which is detrimental to the client (see Hoff's *People in Crisis,* Chapter 5 for in-depth discussion of this clinical management problem).

Further, there may be some individuals for whom the ability to contact the crisis service, primarily through its hotline, may make the difference between maintaining themselves in the community or returning to the hospital. These might include people who suffer from hallucinations and call the service as a way of regaining control and a touchstone on reality. Others might be individuals who suffer from frequent panic attacks, and for whom the ability to connect with a calm, soothing presence, capable of making careful assessment, makes a world of difference.

Some repeat callers to crisis services abuse the line for the purpose of sexual excitation. Most centers have a policy about these calls. For many, it is to deny the caller access to the service while engaged in sexually explicit description or masturbation. Other centers believe that the frequent sexually explicit caller is someone in considerable difficulty and attempt to work with him (it is usually a male). What is important is to provide workers with clear guidelines consistently adhered to by the service (see Wark, 1984, *The Sex Caller and the Telephone Counseling Center*). In fact, consistency is a crucial element in working with ALL clients classified as "chronic," or less pejoratively, as "maintenance."

Data Collection and Utilization

In this computer dominated era, the collection of data is on the minds of most boards of directors and administrators. There are several applicable and useful data collection instruments. Certified crisis centers can be contacted for examples. It is important for the agency to determine what type of information it needs to collect and for what purpose. There is often a strong temptation to collect more than is useful simply because of the capacity to do so. One must examine not only utility, but also the human resources required to maintain data input and analysis.

Complete data provide documentation about the use of the crisis program. Data collection is an effective tool for funders, board members, and staff to understand the nature of the program's work. In addition, an effective data collection mechanism can give the program focus. What populations are not being reached? How does the agency's client population compare to the target group (e.g., if males between the ages of 23 and 30 are the highest risk group for suicide in a given community, but females between the ages of 50 and 59 are the primary group of callers to the agency, this may indicate a need for more effective outreach efforts)? In addition, data can be used to measure the effectiveness of staffing patterns (e.g., Are there periods when the agency should strive to make more staff available?). Also, data can be used to justify certain funding requests, e.g., the appropriateness of youth funds for a service which can document utilization by young people.

The kinds of data useful to collect include sex, age, marital status, current living situation, primary problem, lethality, victimization, intensity of crisis, duration of contact, referral, and employment status. Even here, a particular piece of information should be examined for its significance. For example, in Ithaca, New York for a number of years, employment status was a collected item. Ithaca is a high employment area since education is its primary industry. There is relatively little fluctuation in the unemployment rate, which remains one of the lowest in New York State. Over the years, the data revealed nothing significant. However, subjective impressions were that a number of people were UNDERemployed. A change was made in the data collection to reveal that in this college/university community, there were significant numbers of "captive employees." So, highly qualified spouses of graduate students or faculty who were forced to turn to employment below their level of ability were in a role that generated a special kind of stress.

Data should play a role in shaping the training program. An analysis of statistics will reveal the nature of the presenting problems. Major issues that the agency works with should be part of the initial training program. If a crisis program receives a significant number of calls from mental patients who have been discharged into the community, special attention should be given to understanding their needs. At the same time, one can use data to eliminate from training those issues that do not surface in the program's operation. Furthermore, data can be used for supervisory analysis and program evaluation. A comparison of lethality and duration of contact can indicate if the program is expending its resources on the clients who are at greatest risk.

Evaluation

The centrality of program evaluation

One of the most important uses of data is program evaluation, which should be an integral part of agency functioning. It involves boards of directors, staff, and clients. Evaluation can be rigorous and formal, conducted by an outside agency or internal and informal (Stein and Lambert, 1984). Many agencies are located near universities, rich potential resources for assistance with program evaluation. Graduate students who are under supervision are often looking for a hands-on evaluation project. Their interests can be tailored to fit agency needs for information about itself. Some faculty members have an interest in some aspect of the agency's function and are willing to conduct an evaluation. It may be useful to involve and familiarize a member of a psychology or sociology faculty on the agency's board of directors to introduce new energy and resources for evaluation.

The board of directors may assign the task of program evaluation to its own program committee. Their strategies may include personal interview with relevant staff and representatives of other agencies, review of data indicating utilization and other factors, review of service costs, a written questionnaire, etc. This requires a committed, sensitive, and capable group of volunteers and will probably necessitate one member from the agency's paid staff to serve as a resource person. Measurable program objectives simplify such program evaluation.

Certification of crisis services

One of the most fruitful avenues for assessing the functioning of a crisis service is through the certification process offered by the AAS. Since consumers are increasingly conscious of their desire for appropriate (and many would argue, their right to) service, all crisis trainers and service providers should be aware of this certification program and take steps toward providing service that conforms to national standards.

Besides the humanistic value of assuring minimum standards of service for persons in crisis, other advantages are cited in the AAS *Certification Standards Manual* (Wells and Hoff, 1984):

- AAS certification provides validation of a service delivery program that performs according to nationally recognized standards;

- AAS certification examiners offer consultation tailored to the needs of an individual program, its staff, and its board;
- the increased visibility and credibility of an AAS-certified program provide opportunities for modeling of program excellence to other agencies and professionals;
- AAS certification provides a morale boost for staff working in the newly emerged field of crisis intervention;
- AAS-certified programs have additional credibility with funding agencies and insurance companies;
- programs seeking AAS certification have access to criteria for systematic, ongoing self-evaluation;
- people in life-threatening and other crises obtaining service from AAS-certified programs are assured that staff of these agencies have seriously examined their commitment to provide service according to nationally recognized standards.

Agencies eligible for AAS certification include independent crisis centers, emergency mental health programs operating within community mental health centers, branches of the The Samaritans, various professional psychiatric agencies, and comparable groups offering crisis services. (See Appendix G for the seven Areas and Components of crisis service function that are evaluated by AAS standards.) Further information about this national certification program is available from the AAS Central Office: 2459 S. Ash, Denver, CO 80222; 303–692–0985.

References

Kotkov, B. 1983. "On hiding, reaching out and disclosure." *Psychiatry,* 46:370 – 376.

McGee, R. K., and B. Jennings. 1973. "Ascending to 'lower levels': The case for nonprofessional crisis workers." In D. Lester and G. Brokopp, eds. *Crisis intervention by telephone.* Springfield, IL: Charles C. Thomas.

Stein, D. M., and M. J. Lambert. 1984. "Telephone counseling and crisis intervention: A review." *American Journal of Community Psychology,* 12(1): 101–126.

Walfish, S. 1983. "Crisis telephone counselors' views of clinical interaction situations." *Community Mental Health Journal,* 19(3):219–226.

Wark, V. 1984. *The sex caller and the telephone counseling center.* Springfield, IL: Charles C. Thomas.

Wells, J. O., and L. A. Hoff, eds. 1984. *Certification standards manual.* Denver: American Association of Suicidology.

8

Consultation and Community Education in Crisis Work

Consultation and Community Education ▬▬▬▬▬▬
in the Primary Care Context

In 1978, at the conference in Alma Ata in the Soviet Union, the World Health Organization proclaimed a goal of "health for all by the year 2000." Central to the achievement of this goal is the role of primary health care, of which crisis services, consultation, and community education are pivotal elements. Throughout the world there is growing recognition of the importance of primary care as populations increase while health care resources either remain stable or shrink. Nevertheless, in many countries, the majority of money available for health is allocated to tertiary and secondary care (centered in hospitals) for people who are ill and/or disabled rather than to primary care, which is centered on people who are functioning in their homes and community. Particularly in the United States, a disproportionate percentage of health care dollars is spent on acute care. As a result, insufficient attention is directed toward the prevention of acute episodes in both physical and emotional realms, while the political-economic parameters of primary prevention and crisis risk are almost completely neglected. Such practices and policies supporting them are diametrically opposed to the WHO goal of health for all and to the need to contain escalating health care costs.

Certainly those who are mentally and emotionally disabled should have the public and private care they need. But, there is a twofold irony in the wastefulness of a human service system that does not emphasize primary prevention with other necessary care for the disabled. First, if community education and consultation, with the crisis service described in earlier chapters, were available to all, much human pain in the form of depression, alcohol and other drug abuse, institutionalization, suicide, and violence against others might be avoided. Second, the dollar costs per client of secondary and especially tertiary level of care are much higher than the cost of primary care. It may require several intensive hours of social network intervention to help a worker stay on the job, a child to stay in school, or a person to stay in a home situation rather than be institutionalized. But such crisis service is still much less expensive than the alternatives of unemployment, individual child care, or institutionalization. Figure 8.1 illustrates that primary care is not only the least costly to society and the client, but also preserves the greatest independence of the client in contrast to hospital-based care (Hoff, 1984:18). Ideally, community education, consultation, and crisis training should interface

Figure 8.1

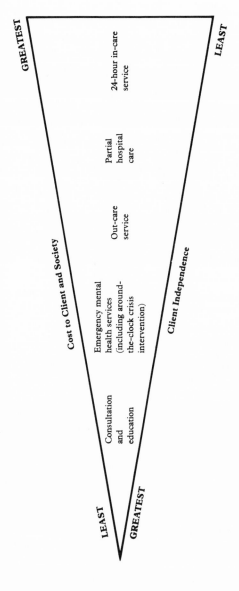

Continuum of Mental Health Services: Cost and Client Independence. Assisting distressed people in their natural social roles (homemaker, paid worker, student) through consultation, education, and crisis services is the *least* costly means of service and allows the *greatest* client independence; institutional-based care is the *most* costly means and allows the *least* client independence.

Originally printed in *People in Crisis*, 2nd ed. (Menlo Park, CA: Addison-Wesley, 1984). Reprinted with permission of publisher.

(Seroka, Knapp, Knight, Siemon, and Starbuck, 1986). For example, an education program for a parent-teacher association regarding crisis and drug use could result in the teachers' requesting regular consultation concerning crises among drug-involved children and adolescents. Or, a community health nurse who receives consultation regarding a suicidal person may request in-service training in crisis intervention for the entire staff.

However, the implementation of such primary care programs is not yet widespread, and the contradiction between ideals and reality persists. One major reason lies in the complex interplay of cultural values and political-economic factors that sustains the emphasis on hospital-based care in spite of its greater cost (McKinlay, 1979). A related problem in the United States, in contrast to Canada, for example, is that 40 million people have no health insurance, in spite of the growth of health maintenance organizations (HMOs).

The neglect of primary care has tremendous implications for crisis educators and administrators. Besides the general challenge of conducting consultation and community education programs, crisis professionals face other major obstacles. Their work is often devalued because it is not usually carried out within mainstream hospital-based contexts. Also, there is often no insurance coverage for the work done. And, the pressure for crisis service is increased by the greater crisis vulnerability of people who lack health insurance. These obstacles and the issues contributing to them underscore the importance of sound consultation and community education programs in the crisis field. The remainder of this chapter presents the general features of such programs and guidelines to develop them systematically into regular features of comprehensive crisis services.

Consultation: Its Nature and Purposes ■■■■■■■■■■

Consultation is an excellent means of assuring that clients in crisis do not suffer because a worker lacks extensive experience in solving complex human problems. In health and general human service fields, consultation has been widely used to bring the fullest possible range of knowledge to bear on a person's particular health problem. In the community mental health movement and in Caplan's (1964) work *Principles of Preventive Psychiatry,* consultation is considered to have an equally important function in the mental health and crisis fields.

In crisis work, consultation can take place between a crisis worker, volunteer or paid, and a designated consultant, between a crisis worker and his or her supervisor, or between a crisis specialist and another service worker such as a nurse, physician, police officer, teacher, pastor, or agency administrator. Many supervisors prefer to function in a consultative role with workers concerning clinical matters, rather than in their appointed authority role as supervisor (see Chapter 7 pp. 96–97 for distinctions between these roles). The exception to this usually occurs when the worker's level of skill is insufficient to allow complete freedom to accept or reject the recommendations of the supervisor, a freedom that characterizes the consultative relationship. The focus of consultation can either be on problems working with an individual client ("case consultation") or on an entire program. Even though case consultation is more common, program consultation might prevent crises and other problems if it were frequently utilized.

The Consultative Relationship

Even though a consultant offers suggestions and recommendations to the consultee, the consultee is free to accept or reject the help offered (except in special instances between a worker and supervisor as noted earlier). However, along with the *freedom* to accept or reject the advice, the consultee has the *responsibility* for the quality of service to the client. If the consultee agrees that certain action should be taken on behalf of a client, it is his or her responsibility to carry it out. Actually, though there is high status in the consultant role, there is no line or "ascribed" authority (as in a supervisory relationship). Instead, a consultant has staff or "achieved" authority, e.g., one's personal wisdom acquired through education and experience, which (it must always be remembered) the consultee can accept or reject. Misunderstanding or non-acceptance of this fact by consultants can be the source of many problems in consultative relationships.

Many of the qualifications of a good supervisor, discussed in Chapter 7, apply to the consulting role. Also, many effective supervisors use a consulting style even though they possess ascribed or line authority over supervisees. In general, it takes time and patience to develop productive consultative relationships with various caregivers and/or administrators. People who take on consultative roles should be very experienced and confident in the crisis field, without appearing arrogant. A superior attitude does little to foster meaningful consultative relationships. No matter how skilled or confident a consultant is, there is always something to be learned from those we consult with and supervise. Consultants should also be sufficiently secure in themselves to sustain possible rejections of advice or recommendations without experiencing severe blows to self-esteem.

A professional degree in a mental health field may or may not be one of the qualifications of an effective consultant. Rather, crisis consultants' success depends on their expertise as crisis workers. Unfortunately, consultants in some suicide prevention and crisis services have had no special training in crisis intervention, suicide, and homicide risk assessment, and many have never made a crisis outreach visit. Crisis workers and the people they serve are bound to be cheated by this kind of consultative arrangement. Extensive knowledge and experience in the crisis field are undisputed means of avoiding many problems in the consultative process.

Depending on the attitude of the consultant, a consultee may find it humiliating or rewarding to work with a consultant on a problem. A crisis worker or administrator should never have to feel inferior or demeaned from the necessity of seeking help from a consultant. If and when this happens, neither the client, the consultee, nor the consultant benefits. Instead, it is useful to view the relationship as an *alliance* for the benefit of the person(s) in crisis. When communication breaks down in consultative relationships, the consultant should assume leadership in trying to resolve the problem.

Criteria and Procedures for ▬▬▬▬▬▬▬▬ Crisis Consultation*

There are many reasons why crisis workers (paid and/or volunteer) and community caretakers should seek consultation. Who, among crisis workers, requires supervision and/or such consultation? Actually, everyone does. This is true at least inasmuch as all workers are accountable to someone:

- executive director to the board of directors,
- crisis workers to a program clinical director, or appointed supervisor,
- all of us to the consumers (people in crisis) whom we serve,
- agency or board of directors to a funding body or to legislators who are accountable to the people who elected them.

* Originally printed in *People in Crisis*, 1st ed. (Menlo Park, CA: Addison-Wesley, 1978). Reprinted with permission of publisher.

In crisis work, there will be many times when we need the support of a colleague, especially in very stressful situations. For example, when dealing with a highly suicidal person, we should always work on a team or consultative basis, even if it is only with a peer. The responsibility and risks involved in doing otherwise are too great. Crisis workers should obtain consultation from a senior level crisis worker in the following kinds of situations:

1. Circumstances where there is significant danger of suicide or homicide.

2. Situations in which medication and/or psychiatric hospitalization may be indicated.

3. Cases with legal or ethical implications, other factors involving the worker and/or agency in court, or other legal or public proceedings.

4. Situations where the client has a grievance about the service received.

5. Cases in which a medical and/or neuropsychiatric diagnosis is needed.

6. Any circumstance where the crisis worker is uncertain about what to do to help the client more effectively.

7. Any situation in which the worker's own issues interfere with an objective response to a client's needs.

Once a worker—crisis counselor, nurse, teacher—has decided that he or she needs consultation, the following steps should be taken:

1. The consultee should clearly define, verbally and in writing, specific questions to be asked of the consultant and explicit information desired or expectation of recommendations concerning specific problems areas.

2. In the instance of case consultation, the consultant and consultee together should determine in a prior conference if the client should be seen directly by the consultant.

3. The consultee prepares the client for a conference with the consultant, if and when such a decision has been reached.

4. The outcomes of the consultation should be recorded on appropriate agency forms.

Case Consultation Illustrations

The following examples illustrate some of the uses of case consultation by crisis workers:

A particular human service worker, in this case a police officer, may wish to provide a service for a person in crisis in which he or she is not particularly skilled.

JEFFREY MONROE

A police officer called a local crisis clinic from the Monroe home when he saw that he was unable to handle Jeffrey Monroe's irrational, upsetting behavior. Although Mr. Monroe was violent, throwing things and breaking furniture, the officer could tell that he was also mentally disturbed. (Mr. Monroe stated that he was afraid that his wife and others were plotting against him.) The crisis worker came to the home and acted as a consultant to the officer who, by this time, had established some rapport with the family. Together, they convinced Mr. Monroe to seek help at an emergency mental health clinic.

A crisis worker wants to obtain a broader perspective and help with a complex crisis situation that involves many people.

JANET ORLEY

Janet Orley, age 29, has diabetes but neglects to take her insulin. She believes it is contaminated after each use of the vial and refuses to let her mother or the community health nurse administer it. Ms. Orley is also picked up occasionally by the police for vagrancy and public intoxication. She has a crisis counselor who has assisted her through several incidents, but without much change in her underlying lifestyle. Ms. Orley refuses psychiatric treatment regarding her irrational ideas about the insulin. One day the nurse called the crisis counselor after discovering Ms. Orley in a diabetic coma. An ambulance was dispatched, and Ms. Orley was hospitalized. When Ms. Orley was over her medical crisis, the crisis counselor sought consultation from the program director of the crisis clinic about the next steps in helping Janet. Among the suggestions that the supervisor made was an interagency planning conference, including Ms. Orley as an active participant.

Someone in a supervisory position needs advice from a crisis specialist concerning a staff problem (Kalafat, 1984), e.g., a hospital supervising nurse, Ms. Johnson, calls a crisis worker for help with a staff member who becomes suicidal. Since the supervisor is personally concerned about the staff member and has her own fears about suicide and death, she wants the help of an outside consultant to avoid an overly subjective approach to dealing with the problem.

A member of the community, perhaps a teacher or community health nurse, wants to gain a broader knowledge base in working with someone who may be suicidal or victimized by crime (Underwood and Fiedler, 1983; Fein and Knaut, 1986). A consultation session is arranged to discuss the case in detail (e.g., the teacher notes that a student is writing essays about suicide) and an agreement reached about the next steps to take (e.g., the nurse or teacher receives suggestions about how to respond to the person's suicidal talk or writing so he or she will feel confident in openly discussing the problem). Subsequent steps for a referral process may be worked out, or the situation may be discussed in a follow-up consultation session, depending on the particular circumstances of the case. Such determining circumstances might be: How much information does the worker already have? How much danger of suicide is there, based on the information available? What other information is needed and what is the best way of obtaining it in order to decide on next steps?

DENNIS FLEETON

Dennis, age 15, was referred by a community mental health agency to a school for disturbed children and adolescents. His grades were passable. He was physically abusive to other children and sometimes struck out at teachers. During one of his fights with another boy, he knocked out both the boy and the teacher who tried to intervene. Dennis was immediately expelled from school. Dennis also had outbursts of uncontrolled behavior at home. While he was on home instruction, the counselor initiated consultation sessions with the school in an effort to get Dennis reinstated. In fact, Dennis' upsets in school coincided with his mother's hospitalization for heart disease.

Family crisis counseling sessions were held along with individual sessions for Dennis. He was able to verbalize many of his fears about his mother's heart disease and possible death. Gradually, he learned how to express his feelings in less destructive ways. After several conferences at school, including Dennis and his parents, Dennis was reinstated. Teachers and the guidance counselor stated that they had learned a great deal about adolescent behavior and the role of the family (in this case, the mother's illness) in an adolescent's problems. The school decided to continue regular consultative sessions with the mental health agency, even though earlier attempts of the agency to establish a regular consultative relationship had been refused.

Program Consultation

Although utilized much less frequently than case consultation, program consultation is also important. However, there is a tendency to wait for a specific crisis before examining an entire program and the institutions that contribute to individual crisis situations. For example, some nursing homes have the practice of a "fruit-basket-upset" staffing arrangement with staff rotating ward assignments biweekly. This kind of programming contributes to the adjustment problems (and possibly crises) of older people whose age makes it difficult to accommodate to such rapid changes. It also prevents older people and staff from establishing stable relationships with one another, which could prevent individual crisis situations. The tendency to focus on individual cases and neglect the preventive approach implied in program consultation conforms to the general inattention to primary care discussed earlier.

The concept of program consultation is often resisted most strongly by the very institutions that could use it most productively, e.g., hospitals, nursing homes, and schools. The most effective way to proceed in these circumstances is through community education efforts and the availability of consultation regarding individual crisis cases. When administrators see the positive results of consultation concerning individual stress situations, they are often more open to the possibility of program consultation. Also, a resistive institution may be more open to program consultation shortly after a crisis has occurred. For example, a psychiatric nurse working as a crisis counselor assisted a nursing home staff in understanding and helping a man who had attacked a nurse and another resident. After this experience, the nursing home administrative staff arranged for a regular consultative program with the mental health agency in which the psychiatric nurse worked.

In general, program consultation is more challenging to the consultant and more threatening to the consultee than is case consultation. This is because more is at stake in the possible exposure of leadership practices, vested interests, and perhaps the continuation of the agency itself if certain deeply-rooted problems are exposed. On the other hand, program consultation can be more rewarding because it leads to the necessary change and revitalization (or continuation if shutdown is threatened) of an entire institution.

Crisis services seeking certification from the AAS report that one of the most beneficial aspects of the process is the program consultation they receive from the certification examiners. Such consultation is built into the feedback session to the agency director (and designated staff) at the conclusion of the certification site visit. Agencies preparing for certification may also arrange for pre-site visit program consultation if necessary.

Community Education ▬▬▬▬▬▬▬▬▬▬▬▬▬▬▬▬▬▬

Since each community member is bound to experience a crisis at some time or will be called on to help someone else in crisis, everyone should know where and how to get community crisis services. A comprehensive community crisis service that meets national standards has a public relations program that gives all citizens this vital information. There should be established channels of communication between community members and various service organizations. One of the AAS standards for crisis services is that citizens have regular input to the board of control and administration. This is one important way to determine how well-informed citizens are about their crisis service. Figure 8.2 suggests target groups that could benefit from various education programs in the crisis field. Citizens should know:

- what services are available,
- how they can get in touch with the crisis service,
- how long it takes to get help in an emergency,
- who is eligible for the service,
- what, if anything, it will cost to use the service (The service should be publicly supported.),
- if the case will be kept confidential.

All citizens should know the answers to these questions. A public relations committee of the community crisis service has several available

Figure 8.2

Target Groups

Mental Health Providers
- Counselors
- Clinical psychologists
- Social workers
- Psychiatric nurses
- Psychiatrists

Health Providers
- Rescue workers
- Nurses
- Physicians
- Victim advocates

Caretakers
- Social service workers
- Clergy
- Teachers, Residential staffs
- Police

Community Service Groups
- Salvation Army
- Travelers aid, International Institute
- Voluntary agencies (Mental Health Association, Help Your Neighbor, Welcome Wagon)
- Youth boards
- Service clubs (Lions, Elks, etc.)
- Bartenders, hairdressers, disc jockeys
- Media (TV, radio, newspapers)

Citizen and Consumer Group
- Town boards, supervisors, councils
- Parent-teacher associations
- Church groups
- Business associations
- Senior citizen clubs
- Citizen boards of human service agencies

Types of Programs
- a
- b
- c
- d
- e

Key
a. General information about crisis service.
b. Consultation concerning specific crisis situations.
c. Community resources and interagency referral system.
d. Crisis management.
e. Special Topics.

* If and when these groups are trained and experienced in crisis management, they should be able to serve as community education, consultants, and trainers for others.

avenues for publicizing the answers. At the same time, the committee can offer information to help people to recognize and understand better the common signs of crisis, to learn how to help themselves and others better through new ways of problem solving, and to improve generally their mental health and avoid destructive ways of problem-solving such as with alcohol and other drug abuse, violence toward others, and suicide attempts.

Some of the basic tasks involved in a community education program are as follows:

1. Appoint a director or coordinator of public relations with experience in crisis intervention and community education work. She or he should select committee members who are willing and able to work on behalf of the service.

2. Identify the specific educational needs of the local community being served. This can be done by contacting board members, citizen advisory and planning groups, town boards, and caretakers such as police, teachers, EMTs and rescue squads, service clubs (Lions, Elks, Rotary, etc.), churches, and other community groups.

3. Develop education materials such as brochures and posters that tell about crises in families, alcohol and other drug use, aging, suicide, AIDS, violence, divorce, illness, and transition states.

4. Organize a systematic means of distributing these materials, e.g., develop working agreements with nurses and physicians for making brochures and business cards available in waiting rooms (e.g., of a local battered women's shelter) and a routine mechanism for replenishing the supply. Churches and service clubs are also good places to distribute crisis information.

5. Organize a speakers bureau with people who can discuss various topics pertinent to crisis intervention. Speakers could appear at service clubs, churches, other community groups, on the local media, and before special groups such as senior citizens and school health and social science classes. Speakers bureau activities can often be developed cooperatively with the local Mental Health Association.

6. Develop a program for systematic and periodic contact with the media. Only 1–3% of the total United States population does not have television, and nearly everyone has a radio. In developing countries, radios are available even in remote rural areas. The Public Relations Committee of the AAS has developed an impressive media kit for promoting public information about suicide and how to get

help in a crisis. NOVA, Women's Centers, police stations, and the YMCA have information about what to do if victimized by crime. These are valuable resources for every public relations coordinator of a crisis service.

7. Work with the local telephone company to assure listing of the crisis service number along with emergency numbers at the front of the directory, if this has not already been done.

8. Develop a system for monitoring and evaluating the outcome of the public relations program. For example, conduct a random survey to find out what percentage of citizens have appropriate information about local crisis services. In Great Britain such a survey revealed that 92% of the population had knowledge of The Samaritans (Bagley, 1968).

A strong community education program not only gives people the information they need about crisis services, but also helps keep the program on a firmer financial foundation. Citizens who are informed and actively involved with a program important to them will make sure that the program makes vital use of their tax dollars.

References

Bagley, C. 1968. "The evaluation of a suicide prevention scheme by an ecological method." *Social Science and Medicine,* 2:1–14.

Caplan, G. 1964. *Principles of preventive psychiatry.* New York:Basic Books.

Fein, E., and S. A. Knaut. 1986. "Crisis intervention and support: Working with police." *Social Casework,* May:276–282.

Hoff, L. A. 1984. *People in crisis.* 2nd ed. Menlo Park, CA: Addison-Wesley.

Kalafat, J. 1984. "Training community psychologists for crisis intervention." *American Journal of Community Psychology,* 12(2):241–251.

McKinlay, J. B. 1979. The case for refocusing upstream: The political economy of illness. In *Patients, physicians, and illness.* 3rd ed. E. G. Jaco, ed. New York: Free Press.

Seroka, C. M., C. Knapp, S. Knight, C. R. Siemon, and S. Starbuck. 1986 "A comprehensive program for postdisaster counseling." *Social Casework,* January:37–44.

Underwood, M. M., and N. Fiedler. 1983. "The crisis of rape: A community response." *Community Mental Health Journal.* (   ):227–230.

Appendix A: Sample Bibliographies

Some Current Crisis Textbooks

Aguilera, D., and D. Messick. 1986. *Crisis intervention.* 4th ed. St. Louis: C. V. Mosby.

Burgess, A. W., and B. A. Baldwin. 1981. *Crisis theory and practice.* Englewood Cliffs, NJ: Prentice-Hall.

Hoff, L. A. 1984. *People in crisis: Understanding and helping.* 2nd ed. Menlo Park, CA: Addison-Wesley.

Janosik, E. H. 1984. *Crisis counseling.* Monterey, CA: Wadsworth Health Sciences Div.

Puryear, D. A. 1980. *Helping people in crisis.* San Francisco: Jossey-Bass.

General Crisis Library

Ackerman, R. J. 1983. *Children of alcoholics: A guidebook for educators, therapists, and parents.* Holmes Beach, FL: Learning Publications.

Action for mental health. 1961. Report of the Joint Commission on Mental Illness and Health. New York: Basic Books.

Alvarez, A. 1973. *The savage god.* New York: Bantam.

Arnold, W. E. 1980. *Crisis communication.* Scottsdale, AZ: Gorsuch Scarisbrick.

Attorney General's Task Force on Family Violence. 1984. *Final report.* Washington, D.C.: U.S. Department of Justice.

Baechler, J. 1979. *Suicide.* New York: Basic Books.

Battin, M. P., and D. J. Mayo, eds. 1980. *The philosophical issues.* New York: St. Martin's Press.

Berkley, G. E. 1981. *The craft of public administration.* Boston: Allyn & Bacon.

Bograd, M. 1984. "Family systems approaches to wife battering: A feministcritique." *American Journal of Orthopsychiatry*, 54(4):558–568.

Bolton, I. 1983. *My Son . . . My Son. . . .* Belmore Way, NE: Bolton Press.

Borck, L. E., and S. B. Fawcett. 1982. *Learning counseling and problem-solving skills.* New York: Haworth Press.

Borg, S., and J. Lasker. 1981. *When pregnancy fails.* Boston: Beacon Press.

Browmiller, S. 1975. *Against our will.* New York: Simon & Schuster.

Burgess, A. W., and L. L. Holstrom. 1974. *Rape: Victims of crisis.* Bowie, MD: Robert J. Brady Co.

Cain, A. C., ed. 1972. *Survivors of suicide.* Springfield, IL: Charles C. Thomas.

Caine, L. 1974. *Widow.* New York: William Morrow & Co.

Calhoun, L. G., J. W. Selby, and H. E. King. 1976. *Dealing with crisis: A guide to critical life problems.* Englewood Cliffs, NJ: Prentice-Hall.

Campbell, J., and J. Humphreys. 1984. *Nursing care of victims of violence.* Reston, VA: Reston Publishing Co.

Caplan, G. 1964. *Principles of preventive psychiatry.* New York: Basic Books.

Carkhuff, R. R. 1972. *The art of helping.* Amherst, MA: Human Resource Development Press.

———. 1973. *The art of problem solving.* Amherst, MA: Human Resource Development Press.

Clark, D. 1977. *Loving someone gay.* New York: New American Library.

Cohen, L. H., W. Clairborn, and G. A. Specter. 1983. *Crisis intervention.* 2nd ed. New York: Behavioral Publications.

Coleman, J. C. 1980. *The nature of adolescence.* New York: Methuen & Co.

Coleman, L. 1987. *Suicide clusters.* Boston and London Faber & Faber.

Crary, E. 1979. *Without spanking or spoiling.* Seattle: Parenting Press.

Cutter, F. 1984. *Suicide prevention triangle.* Chicago: Nelson-Hall.

Delworth, U., E. H. Rudow, and J. Taub. 1972. *Crisis intervention/hotline: A guidebook to beginning and operating.* Springfield, IL: Charles C. Thomas.

Douglas, J. D. 1967. *The social meanings of suicide.* New York: Princeton University Press.

Dublin, L. I. 1963. *Suicide: A sociological and statistical study.* New York: Ronald Press.

Dunn. E. J., J. L. McIntosh, and K. Dunne-Maxim, eds. 1987. *Suicide and its aftermath: Understanding and counseling the survivors.* New York: W. W. Norton.

Durkheim, E. 1951. *Suicide: A study in sociology.* New York: Free Press. (First published in 1897.)

Erickson, E. 1963. *Childhood and society.* 2nd ed. New York: W. W. Norton.

Everstine, D. S., and Everstine, L. 1983. *People in crisis: Strategic therapeutic interventions.* New York: Brunner/Mazel.

Farberow, N. L. 1980. *The many faces of suicide.* New York: McGraw-Hill.

Farberow, N. L., ed. 1975. *Suicide in different cultures.* Baltimore: University Park Press.

———, ed. 1980. *The many faces of death.* New York: McGraw-Hill.

Farberow, N. L., and E. S. Shneidman, eds. 1961. *The cry for help.* New York: McGraw-Hill.

Faucher, E. 1985. *Surviving.* New York: Scholastic.

Feifel, H., ed. 1959. *The meaning of death.* New York: McGraw-Hill.

———, ed. 1977. *New meanings of death.* New York: McGraw-Hill.

Finkelhor, D., R. J. Gelles, G. T. Hotaling, and M. A. Straus. 1983. *The dark side of families: Current family violence research.* Beverly Hills, CA: Sage Publications.

Giffin, M. 1983. *A cry for help.* New York: Doubleday & Co.

Gil, D. G. 1970. *Violence against children.* Cambridge, MA: Harvard University Press.

Giovacchini, P. 1981. *The urge to die: Why do young people commit suicide.* New York: MacMillan Publishing Co.

Golan, N. 1978. *Treatment in crisis situations.* New York: Free Press.

———. 1981. *Passing through transitions.* New York: Free Press.

Gooderham, H. 1984. "Let's talk special report on inmate suicide." In *Let's Talk—The Correctional Service of Canada,* 9(20): 1–4. Canada.

Goodman, L. M. 1981. *Death and the creative life.* New York: Springer Publishing Co.

Gorton, J. G., and R. Partridge, eds. 1980. *Practice and management of psychiatric emergency care.* St. Louis: C. V. Mosby.

Greenspan, M. 1983. *A new approach to women and therapy.* New York: McGraw-Hill.

Greenstone, J. L., and S. Leviton. 1981. *Hotline: Crisis intervention directory.* New York: Facts on File.

Grollman, E. A. 1971. *Suicide: prevention, intervention, Postvention.* Boston: Beacon Press.

Hansell, N. 1976. *The person in distress.* New York: Human Sciences Press.

Harper, R. A. 1975. *The new psychotherapies.* Englewood Cliffs, NJ: Prentice-Hall.

Hatton, C., S. Valente, and A. Rink. 1984. *Suicide: Assessment and intervention.* 2nd ed. New York: Appleton-Century-Crofts.

Hendin, H. 1982. *Suicide in America.* New York: W. W. Norton.

Herman, J. 1981. *Father-daughter incest.* Cambridge, MA: Harvard University Press.

Hewett, J. H. 1980. *After suicide.* Philadelphia: Westminster Press.

Hill, W. H. 1984. Intervention and postvention in schools. In Sudak, H.S. *Suicide in the young,* (pp. 407–416). Littleton, MA: John Wright.

Hoff, L. A. 1984. *People in crisis: Understanding and helping.* 2nd ed. Menlo Park, CA: Addison-Wesley.

Jacobson, G. F. 1980. "Crisis intervention in the 1980's." In *New Direction for Mental Health Services,* 6.

James, M., and D. Jongeward. 1971. *Born to win: Transactional analysis with gestalt experiments.* Reading, MA.:Addison-Wesley.

Joan, P. 1986. *Preventing teenage suicide: The living alternative handbook.* New York: Human Sciences Press.

Kastenbaum, R., and R. Aisenberg. 1972. *The psychology of death.* New York: Springer Publishing Co.

Kennedy, E. 1977. *On becoming a counselor: A basic guide for non-professional counselors.* New York: Seabury Press.

Kiev, A. 1975. *The courage to live.* New York: Thomas Y. Cromwell.

Kleinberg, S. 1980. *Alienated affections.* New York: St. Martin's Press.

Klyver, N., and M. Reiser. 1983. "Crisis intervention in law enforcement." *The counseling Psychologist,* 11(2): 49 –54.

Krementz, J. 1981. *How it feels when a parent dies.* New York: Alfred A. Knopf.

Kubler-Ross, E. 1969. *On death and dying.* New York: MacMillan Publishing Co.

————. 1982. *Working it through*. New York: MacMillan Publishing Co.

Kushner, H. S. 1981. *When bad things happen to good people*. New York: Schocken Books.

LeShan, E. 1976. *Learning to say good-bye when a parent dies*. New York: Avon Books.

Lester, D., and G. Brockopp, eds. 1973. *Crisis intervention and counseling by telephone*. Springfield, IL: Charles C. Thomas.

Lester, G., and D. Lester. 1971. *Suicide: The gamble with death*. Englewood Cliffs, NJ: Prentice-Hall.

List, J. A. 1980. *The day the loving stopped*. New York: Fawcett Juniper Books.

McGee, R. K. 1974. *Crisis intervention in the community*. Baltimore: University Park Press.

McWhirter, D. P., and A. Mattison. 1984. *The male couple: How relationships develop*. Englewood Cliffs, NJ: Prentice-Hall.

Mackinson, F., ed. 1978. *Pocket guide to chemical hazards*. Washington, D.C.: U.S. Government Printing Office.

Maris, R. W. 1981. *Pathways to suicide: A survey of self-destructive behaviors*. Baltimore: Johns Hopkins University Press.

Maslach, C. 1982. *Burnout: The cost of caring*. Englewood Cliffs, NJ: Prentice-Hall.

Maslow, A. 1970. *Motivation and personality*. 2nd ed. New York: Harper & Row.

Menninger, K. 1938. *Man against himself*. New York: Harcourt, Brace & World.

Miller, J. B. 1976. *Toward a new psychology of women*. Boston: Beacon Press.

Miller, M. 1979. *Suicide after sixty*. New York: Springer Publishing Co.

————. 1984. *Training workshop manual*. San Diego: Suicide Information Center.

Monahan, J. 1981. *The clinical prediction of violent behavior*. Rockville, MD: National Institute of Mental Health.

Morrice, J. K. W. 1976. *Crisis intervention: Studies in community care*. New York: Pergamon Press.

Motto, J. A., C. P. Ross, and N. H. Allen. 1974. *Standards for suicide prevention and crisis centers*. New York: Behavioral Publications.

Myrick, R. D., and T. Erney. 1978. *Caring and sharing: Becoming a peer facilitator*. Minneapolis: Educational Media.

————. 1979. *Youth helping youth: A handbook for training peer facilitators.* Minneapolis: Educational Media.

NiCarthy, G. 1986. *Getting free: Handbook for women in abusive relationships.* rev. ed. Seattle: Seal Press.

Okun, B. 1976. *Effective helping: Interviewing and counseling techniques.* Boston: Duxbury Press.

O'Neil, N., and G. O'Neil. 1974. *Shifting gears: Finding security in a changing world.* New York: M. Evans & Co.

Parad, H. J., ed. 1965. *Crisis intervention: Selected readings.* New York: Family Service Association of America.

Parkes, C. M. 1975. *Bereavement: Studies of grief in adult life.* Middlesex, England: Penguin Books.

Peck, M. L. 1985. Crisis intervention treatment with chronically and acutely suicidal adolescents. In Peck, M. L., N. L. Farberow, and R. E. Litman, eds., *Youth Suicide* (pp.112–122). New York: Springer Publishing Co.

Perlin, S. 1975. *A handbook for the study of suicide.* New York: Oxford University Press.

Pizzey, E. 1977. *Scream silently or the neighbors will hear.* Hillside, NJ: Enslow Publishers.

Portwood, D. 1978. *Common-sense suicide.* New York: Dodd, Mead & Co.

President's Task Force on Victims of Crime. 1982. *Final report.* Washington, D.C.: U.S. Government Printing Office.

Priestley, P., and J. McGuire. 1983. *Learning to help.* London: Tavistock Publications.

Puryear, D. A. 1980. *Helping people in crisis.* San Francisco: Jossey-Bass.

Ramsey, R. F. 1983. *A suicide prevention training program: Trainer's handbook.* Calgary: Suicide Prevention Training Program (SPTP).

Resnik, H. L. P. 1968. *Suicidal behaviors: Diagnosis and management.* Boston: Little, Brown & Co.

Resnik, H. L. P., H. L. Ruben, and D. D. Ruben. 1975. *Emergency psychiatric care.* Philadelphia: Charles Press Publishers.

Rosenthal, T. 1973. *How could I not be among you?* New York: G. Braziller.

Russell, D. E. H. K. 1982. *Rape in marriage.* New York: Collier Books.

Ryan, W. 1971. *Blaming the victim.* New York: Vintage Books.

Sheehy, G. 1976. *Passages.* New York: E. P. Dutton.

Shneidman, E. S. 1969. *On the nature of suicide.* San Francisco: Jossey-Bass.

————. 1972. *Death and the college student.* New York: Behavioral Publications.

————. 1973. *The death of man.* New York: Quadrangle.

————. 1973. *Essays in self-destruction.* New York: Sciences House.

————. 1976. *Suicidology: Contemporary developments.* New York: Grune & Stratton.

Shneidman, E. S., and N. L. Farberow, eds. 1957. *Clues to suicide.* New York: McGraw-Hill.

Shneidman, E. S., N. L. Farberow, and R. Litman. 1970. *The psychology of suicide.* New York: Science House.

Small, L. 1979. *The briefer psychotherapies.* New York: Brunner/Mazel, Publishers.

Speck, R., and C. Attneave. 1973. *Family networks.* New York: Pantheon.

Stark, E., A. Flitcraft, and W. Frazier. 1979. "Medicine and patriarchal violence: The social construction of a 'private' event." *International Journal of Health Services,* 9:461–493.

Straus, M. A., R. J. Gelles, and S. K. Steinmetz. 1980. *Behind closed doors: Violence in the American family.* New York: Anchor Books.

Surgeon General's Workshop on Violence and Public Health. 1986. *Report.* Washington, D.C.: U.S. Department of Public Health (HHS).

Switzer, D. K. 1974. *The minister as crisis counsellor.* Nashville: Abingdon.

Tavris, C. 1983. *Anatomy of anger.* New York: Simon & Schuster.

Washburn, C. K., coor. 1975. *Women in transition.* New York: Charles Scribner's Sons.

Watts, C. A. H. 1980. *Defeating depression: A guide for depressed people and their families.* Rochester, VT: Thorsons Publishers Ltd.

Watzlawick, P. 1983. *The situation is hopeless, but not serious.* New York: W. W. Norton.

Weil, A., and W. Rosen. 1983. *Chocolate to morphine: Understanding mind-active drugs.* Boston: Houghton Mifflin Co.

Weiss, R. 1979. *Going it alone.* New York: Basic Books.

Weissberg, M. P. 1983. *Dangerous secrets: Maladaptive responses to stress.* New York: W. W. Norton.

Weissman, A. D. 1972. *On dying and denying.* New York: Behavioral Publications.

Wells, J. O., and L. A. Hoff, eds. 3rd ed. 1984. *Certification standards manual.* Denver: American Association of Suicidology.

Wetzel, J. W. 1984. *Clinical handbook of depression.* New York: Gardner Press.

Wicks, R. J. 1979. *Helping others: Way of listening, sharing, and counseling.* Radnor, PA: Chilton Book Co.

Wilhite, M. J., and A. P. Ferguson. 1979. "Crisis intervention marathon: A teaching strategy." *Journal of Psychiatric Nursing and Mental Health Services,* 17(2): 25–29.

Worden, J. W. 1982. *Grief counseling and grief therapy.* New York: Springer Publishing Co.

Young, L. A., L. Young, M. Klein, D. Klein, and D. Beyer. 1977. *Recreational drugs.* New York: MacMillan Publishing Co.

Some Literary Sources Dealing with Life Crises

Agee, J. 1971. *A death in the family.* New York: Bantam Books.

Allende, I. 1986. *The house of the spirits.* New York: Bantam Books.

Atwood, M. 1986. *The handmaids tale.* Boston: Houghton Mifflin.

Baldwin, J. 1984. *Notes of a native son.* Boston: Beacon Press.

———. 1985. *Go tell it·on a mountain.* New York: Dell Books.

Banks, R. 1985. *Continental drift.* New York: Harper & Row.

Brooker, A. 1985. *Hotel Deluc.* New York: Pantheon.

Doctorow, E. L. 1971. *The book of Daniel.* New York: Random House.

Erdrich, L. 1985. *Love medicine.* New York: Bantam Books.

Forster, E. M. 1981. *A passage to India.* Cutchogue, NY: Buccaneer Books.

Gordimer, N. 1982. *July's people.* New York: Penguin Books.

Grau, S. A. 1985. *The keepers of the house.* New York: Avon Books.

Hardy, T. 1978. *Tess of D'Urbervilles.* New York: Penguin Books.

Kennedy, W. 1984. *Ironweed.* New York: Penguin Books.

Lowry, M. 1984. *Under the volcano.* New York: Harper & Row.

Mason, B. A. 1985. *In country.* New York: Harper & Row.

Sexton, A. 1982. *Complete Poems*. Boston: Houghton Mifflin.

Shange, N. 1980. *For colored girls who have considered suicide when the rainbow is enuf*. New York: Bantam Books.

Stegner, W. 1979. *All the little live things*. Lincoln, NE: University of Nebraska Press.

Stein, J., with G. Plimpton. 1982. *Edie*. New York: Knopf.

Steinbeck, J. 1986. *The grapes of wrath*. New York: Viking Books.

Styron, W. 1982. *Sophie's choice*. New York: Bantam Books.

Tolstoy, L. 1950. *Anna Karenina*. New York: Random House.

Tolstoy, L. 1983. *The death of Ivan Illyich*. Philadelphia, PA: Porcupine Printing.

Walker, A. 1982. *The color purple*. San Diego, CA: Harcourt, Brace and Jovanovich.

Appendix B: Sample Course Syllabi and Continuing Education Programs

Undergraduate College Courses for ▇▇▇▇▇▇▇▇▇▇▇▇▇
Health and Human Service Professional Students (from
Northeastern University, Boston, MA)

Life crises: Analysis ▇▇▇▇▇▇▇▇▇▇▇▇▇▇▇▇▇
and response (classroom, four quarter hours)

COURSE DESCRIPTION

This interdisciplinary course concerns personal, family, and community crises identified from literature, health agency clientele, and student sources. Concepts from crisis theory, psychology, nursing, sociology, anthropology, and social psychology are used to assess critically the individual's experience of crisis, and the approaches used by providers in human service systems to help people in crisis (e.g., at times of death, divorce, job loss, illness, rape, suicide attempt, and disaster).

RATIONALE

Crises are inherent to life. Response to our own and others' crises can help determine if we grow, stagnate, become emotionally disturbed, or die by our own hand or from the violence of others. All of us pass through the potentially critical stages of human development from birth to death. In traditional societies, individuals are assisted through life's natural transition points by rites of passage embedded in a community's support network. Industrialized societies by comparison have minimal sources of social support for their members during developmental transition states.

132

The structure of urban family life often leaves individuals more alone and vulnerable during various situational crises, e.g., diagnosis of a terminal illness, divorce, victimization by crime, attempted suicide by a family member or friend, disaster, and various community upheavals. Accordingly, many persons experiencing extreme stress and crisis come to medical or mental health institutions. In such settings, life crises are customarily viewed in a psychopathology framework, even though some of these crises may have originated from sociocultural or political sources. Accordingly, the individual receives drugs and a psychiatric label instead of the social support and change strategies indicated for constructive crisis' resolution. Iatrogenic illness is one of the serious implications of this medical approach to life crises (doctor or other health provider-precipitated disabilities, e.g., drug dependency).

This course assumes that concepts and practice strategies around life crises constitute core content for all health providers—nurses, physicians, and others. Also, consumers need knowledge about crisis and intervention strategies to assess the adequacy of providers' response to them and their families. This course is intended, therefore, as an opportunity for students in consumer and/or health and human service provider roles to examine critically the meaning of life crises in a social-cultural versus psychopathological framework and to explore principles and creative strategies that might be used in responding constructively to crises in their own lives, or in their experience as health or human service workers.

COURSE OBJECTIVES

Unit I   Understanding the Crisis Experience.
1. Clarify theoretical approaches and attitudes that can help or hinder creative responses to crisis.
2. Explore the social-psychological, cultural, political, and environmental factors affecting the development and outcome of crisis states.

Content—This Unit surveys the origins, development, and meaning of life crises using examples from anthropology, sociology, literature (e.g., Tolstoy), and students' personal and/or professional experience. Social/human developmental models are critically compared and contrasted with medical or psychopathological models of crisis.

Unit II   The Stress-Crisis-Illness Interrelationship—Assessment and Prevention.

1. Critically examine approaches for assessing stress and crisis states in self and others.
2. Discuss the relevance of assessment for preventing negative crisis outcomes and reducing risk of illness and injury to self or others.

Content—This Unit focuses on approaches to identify crisis states in self and others and distinguish these from acute and insidious stress and illness states, with a view to preventing crises when possible. The assessment process, the concept of "medicalization," psychiatric labeling, and "labeling theory" are critically examined for their relevance in understanding various responses to crisis in contemporary American society, e.g., prescription of tranquilizers to survivors following death of a family member. Case examples are cited from literature and the personal and professional experience of students and instructor.

Unit III   Principles and Strategies for Successful Crisis Management.
1. Compare and contrast social-psychological, nursing, and medical models of crisis intervention and management.
2. Explore various strategies for crises' management and resolution that correspond to the social nature, varied needs, and cultural meaning systems of people in crisis.

Content—This Unit explores the comparative advantages and disadvantages of various models of crisis intervention and management, building on the critique of concepts and assessment approaches identified in Unit II. Crisis management approaches from a social/human developmental perspective are discussed in relation to life crisis situations identified by students or from films and literature.

Unit IV   Life-Threatening Responses to Crisis—Assessment and Intervention.
1. Explore ethical and legal issues relating to the right to die and to intervene during critical life events.
2. Critically examine assessment and intervention techniques for persons in life-threatening situations, e.g., suicide attempts or violent attack of others.

Content—This Unit focuses on ethical issues during life crises and on assessment and intervention approaches to life-threatening situations such as suicide attempts, child abuse, and wife battering. Concepts from critical theory and the sociology of knowledge are used to examine the relative merits of medicalized versus social approaches to these life crises.

Unit V Social Approaches to Personal, Family, and Community Crises.

1. Examine social network principles and strategies applicable to individuals and families in acute crisis situations in home, school, health agency, or community settings.

2. Explore the role of team relationships, consultation, and referral for effective crisis management in health and human service practice settings.

3. Discuss strategies appropriate to personal, family, and community crises (including disaster) originating from natural, cultural, and political-economic sources.

4. Discuss and compare approaches to various life crises in cross-cultural perspective, e.g., assistance during birth, passage through adolescence, and death.

Content—This Unit is built on earlier explorations of the social/human developmental model of crisis and suggests intervention and management approaches based on this model, e.g., social network, team, and consultation concepts and strategies. Social and political action to reduce the crisis vulnerability of certain social groups (e.g., the elderly, women, ethnic minorities, workers and residents exposed to hazardous waste, etc.) are also discussed.

INSTRUCTIONAL APPROACH

Instructional methods include lecture and discussion emphasizing critical analysis of crisis situations from the literature, personal and professional experience, and films. Assigned readings, critique from text, and selected bibliography are also used. The mixture of students in both consumer and provider roles is expected to provide a forum simulating the ideal of service provision around life crises, i.e., a healthy exchange between people in crisis and various professionals from whom they seek assistance and recognition of the complementarity that should prevail around "natural" and "formal" crisis management. Reading and discussion guides are provided for each unit.

REQUIRED TEXTS

Hoff, L. A. 1984. *People in crisis*. 2nd ed. Menlo Park, CA: Addison-Wesley.

Tolstoy, L. *Anna Karenina*. A 19th century classic in paperback.

PARTIAL BIBLIOGRAPHY

Antonovsky, A. 1980. *Health, stress and coping.* San Francisco: Jossey-Bass.

Battin, M. P., and D. J. Mayo, eds. 1980. *Suicide: The philosophical issues.* New York: St. Martin's Press.

Belle, D., ed. 1982. *Lives in stress.* Beverly Hills: Sage Publications.

Fried, N. N., and M. H. Fried. 1980. *Transitions: Four rituals in eight cultures.* New York: W. W. Norton.

Gibbs, L. 1982. *Love canal—my story.* Albany: State University of New York Press.

Goodman, L. 1981. *Death and the creative life.* New York: Springer.

Hansell, N. 1976. *The person in distress.* New York: Human Sciences Press.

Rosenthal, T. 1973. *How could I not be among you?* New York: G. Braziller.

Tolstoy, L. 1960. *The death of Ivan Illyich.* New York: New American Library.

Wijkman, A., and L. Timberlake. 1984. *Natural disasters: Acts of God or acts of man?* London and Washington, D.C.: International Institute for Environment and Development.

EVALUATION

Course evaluation is based on the following:

1. Paper (25%) will be a critical analysis (four or five pages) of a life crisis taken from the newspaper, a film or book, or one's personal or professional experience. Your analysis should draw on at least six readings annotated at the end of the paper. (An annotated bibliography contains a sentence stating what the article is about, a couple of sentences on its relevance to your paper, and a summarizing statement including your recommendations regarding the article, e.g., students with certain interests or every crisis worker should read it, etc.) For example, a relative has a heart attack or needs to be placed in a nursing home, a friend has a crippling car accident, or a classmate becomes suicidal or is raped. As you analyze this life crisis, demonstrate your understanding of key concepts in crisis theory. If a relative was given a tranquilizer following death of a loved one instead of being assisted through "grief work," the "medicalization" of life crises is implied. If you or a family member were in crisis, analyze the extent to which the steps of natural and formal crisis management (Hoff, p. 28 & ff.) were carried out. You might

also see Hoff and Resing "Was This Suicide Preventable?" (AJN, July 1982) for an example of critical case analysis using criteria for suicide risk assessment.

- Topic due for this paper—first class after mid-term,
- Annotated bibliography and final title for this paper due—beginning of second last week of course,
- Paper due—beginning of last week of course.

2. Short assignments around class topics 15%.
3. Mid-term examination 10%.
4. Final examination 25%.
5. Class participation/Self evaluation 25%.

These projects are open to revision, depending on needs and interests of students.

Crisis management practicum (clinical settings, two quarter hours)

COURSE DESCRIPTION

The course includes supervised experience in strategies to assess clients and to plan, implement, and evaluate appropriate service for individuals and families in crisis. A seminar for analysis of student's experiences is also included. The setting for this experience can be any health or social service agency where the student is currently employed, is placed for other experiences, or has the opportunity to assume the role of formal crisis manager. "Crisis Management" in this course is defined as the entire process of working through a crisis to its endpoint of crisis resolution. "Crisis intervention" is one aspect of crisis management carried out by a crisis worker, e.g., a nurse or police officer. The course is intended for any student or practitioner in part- or full-time contact with people in crisis, e.g., physician, nurse, pastor, psychologist, social worker, police officer, or trainee in these disciplines.

PLACEMENT

Junior, senior, or graduate students in health sciences, human services, and programs, e.g., nursing, educational counseling, rehabilitation counseling, criminal justice.

PREREQUISITES

- Current or recent enrollment in the Course: Life Crisis: Analysis and Response.
- Satisfactory achievement in the basic principles and practice strategies in respective disciplines, e.g., nursing.

COURSE OBJECTIVES

Upon completion of this course, the student will be able to:

- select and assess a client in actual or potential crisis,
- develop a plan for assisting the identified client or family in crisis,
- implement a service plan on behalf of individuals or families in crisis, including, possibly, referral,
- evaluate the crisis management strategies carried out from the perspective of client function before and after crisis intervention,
- consider avenues for applying crisis assessment and management techniques in a variety of settings and situations.

COURSE CONTENT

This course contains four major components.

1. General observations of a setting frequented by people in actual or potential emotional crisis, e.g., hospital emergency centers, various inpatient settings, schools, detention centers, and community health clinics.
2. Student's direct experience with people in actual or potential crisis.
3. Student's systematic analysis of number two in writing and conference with the clinical instructor/supervisor.
4. This experience shared in a seminar with other students and the clinical instructor/supervisor.

METHODS OF INSTRUCTION

Students will be helped as necessary to select a client or family for systematic crisis assessment, service planning, and crisis management. The clinical instructor will be available either on-site or by telephone as a resource and guide during the various phases of the crisis management process. Written service and student analysis are critiqued by the instructor leading the seminar's group discussion of clinical practice situations.

Crisis Workers in Indigenous Crisis Centers (an excerpt from SPCS, Inc., Ithaca, NY)

SPCS training curriculum and suggested readings

Please note: Trainees are required to read the material in this manual *before* the session at which time the material will be discussed and should come to the training class with questions and concerns raised by the readings.

First session—introduction

OBJECTIVES

1. To develop a climate of trust and intimacy with other trainees.
2. To discuss the agency's goals and programs.
3. To discuss ethical issues related to training and work in the agency.
4. To explore and clarify the trainer's and trainees' expectations for the training program.

CONTENT

1. Introduction of group members.
2. Housekeeping details for training class.
3. Contract.
4. Confidentiality and ethics.
5. How to give feedback.
6. Group sharing experience.

METHODS

1. Dyad interviews and introduction of partner to group.
2. Outline of housekeeping details and discussion of contract for training period.
3. Lecture presenting overview of the agency.
4. Discussion of confidentiality and ethics, using examples.
5. Model role-play on how to give feedback.
6. Group building exercise (happy/sad or family crest).

READING

Required Introduction and training sections of SPCS manual.
Recommended *Crisis Intervention in the Community* by Richard McGee, Parts I & III; *People in Crisis* by Lee Ann Hoff, 2nd ed., Chapter 1.

Second session—listening communication skills ▬▬

OBJECTIVES

1. To demonstrate basic active listening skills, including reflection of content and feelings.
2. To demonstrate the difference between open and closed questions, and when each is appropriate; to explore the use of invitations and door-openers.
3. To identify the most common communication road blocks.
4. To develop strategies for screening out inappropriate personal disclosure and personal judgement and bias.
5. To discuss the crisis intervention model and the way counseling skills fit into steps of the model.

CONTENT

1. Goals and definitions of active listening.
2. Kind and uses of questions.
3. Empathy, genuineness, and warmth.
4. Other counseling techniques.
5. Personal biases screened out.
6. The crisis intervention model and its relation to counseling skills.

METHODS

1. Communication circle.
2. Lecture and diagram of active listening.
3. Stimulus-response statements.
4. Circle game to practice reflective responses.
5. Lecture on the use of questions.
6. Role-plays in triads.
7. Analysis of the crisis intervention model.
8. Role-plays.

READING

Required Communication section in manual.
Recommended *The Helping Interview* by Alfred Benjamin; *The Skilled Helper* by Gerald Egan; *The Art of Helping* by Carkhuff; *Effective Helping and Interviewing* by Barbara Okun.

Third session—crisis

OBJECTIVES

1. To demonstrate mastery of a working definition of crisis.
2. To identify the characteristics, development, and states of a crisis.
3. To identify how crisis intervention differs from other forms of counseling and/or treatment.
4. To relate the crisis intervention model to this understanding of crisis.

CONTENT

1. Definition of coping mechanisms.
2. Definition of crisis, operational and experiential.
3. Characteristics, development, and stages of crisis; general developmental patterns in crisis.
4. Kinds of crises.
5. Use of the crisis intervention model.

METHODS

1. Discussion of coping mechanisms with examples from group.
2. Guided fantasy.
3. Development of definition of crisis and discussion.
4. Discussion of Hoff's paradigm.
5. Dyad discussion of personal crisis.
6. Role-plays.

READING

Required Crisis section of manual. *People in Crisis* by Lee Ann Hoff, Chapter 2.
Recommended *Crisis Intervention and Counseling by Telephone* by Lester and Brockopp; *Crisis Intervention* by Aquilera and Messick.

Crisis Management— ▬▬▬▬▬▬▬▬▬▬▬▬▬
A Police Academy (a course excerpt overview prepared for Boston Police Academy by Lee Ann Hoff)

Crisis management ▬▬▬▬▬▬▬▬▬▬▬▬▬

DESCRIPTION

This course includes the required principles and techniques for helping people in crisis. The course's focus will be to assess and understand the person or family in crisis, to prevent escalation of crises resulting in possible injury to self and others, and implement a crisis management plan, including the referral and follow-up process. There will be formal presentations, problem solving through small group discussion utilizing case material, critique of audio-visual material, role-playing, guided reading, and field experience emphasizing community linkage networks in crisis work.

GENERAL OBJECTIVES

Participants in the course will:

1. Define their roles in a community-wide system of responsibility for assistance to persons or families in crisis.
2. Examine attitudes and value orientations that affect the development and outcomes of crises.
3. Identify and practice communication skills necessary for effective crisis work.
4. Identify the elements of the crisis situation as a basis for assessment.
5. Apply crisis assessment techniques in simulated and real case situations.
6. Demonstrate skills in crisis management for individuals and families in crisis.
7. Apply crisis assessment and management skills for the self-destructive and violent person.
8. Demonstrate an understanding of the referral, consultation, and social network process in effective crisis management.

COURSE CONTENT

Part I   Basic Elements of Crisis Management.
Unit 1—Introduction, background considerations in crisis work.

1. Definitions—stress, crisis, conflict, emergency, and crisis intervention.
2. Identification of service needs.
3. Types of services available from public and private resources.
4. Role of police in crisis work

   - determining limits for police action,
   - interface of police crisis work with other community resources,
   - explaining limits of police capabilities,
   - identifying hazards and avoiding danger to self and others.

5. Basic tools for effective crisis work

   - attitudes and how they influence crisis outcomes,
   - values and cultural factors in crisis work,
   - communication skills—verbal and non-verbal.

   Unit 2—Elements of the crisis situation.

1. Crisis experience and basic human needs.
2. Components of the crisis state.
3. Manifestations of crisis—feelings, thoughts, and behavior.
4. Outcomes of crisis

   - effective crisis coping and growth,
   - ineffective crisis coping including suicide, assault, and mental illness.

5. Identification of abnormal behavior.
6. Information gathering, assessment of crisis situations, and abnormal behavior.

   Unit 3—Destructive responses to crisis.

1. Dynamics of conflict, power, and force.
2. Dynamic and social factors in self-destructiveness.
3. Signs that help predict suicide.
4. Signs that help predict assaultiveness.
5. Self-destruction through drugs and alcohol.

Unit 4—Crisis and conflict resolution.

1. Planning and gathering resources for conflict resolution.
2. Techniques for crisis and conflict management.
3. Defusing highly-charged individuals and taking control:

   - gaining entry,
   - taking control,
   - distracting techniques,
   - applying physical crisis intervention techniques when necessary,
   - using attitudes and communication to prevent injury.

4. Problem-solving techniques.
5. Consultation, referral and follow-up.

Unit 5—Crisis and conflict resolution. (continued)

1. Techniques of intervention with people threatening or attempting suicide.
2. Techniques of intervention to prevent assault or homicide.
3. Assistance to the child abuse victim or battered spouse.
4. Evaluation of and assistance to rape victims.
5. Management of intoxicated persons.
6. Legal issues in cases of abuse or other crises (e.g., child, rape, runaway, drug and alcohol)
7. Social network techniques and interagency collaboration in crisis and conflict management.

Total Classroom Hours   33

Continuing Education Workshop— ▅▅▅▅▅▅▅▅▅
The Suicidal Person: Prevention, Crisis Intervention, and Follow-up

DESCRIPTION

This one-day workshop focuses on the attitudes, understanding, and skills needed to help the person in suicidal crisis or chronically self-destructive, with an emphasis on application of these attitudes, concepts, and skills in the participants' everyday work with self-destructive people.

OBJECTIVES

1. Assess the potential impact of personal feelings and attitudes in working with suicidal or chronically self-destructive individuals.
2. Analyze clinical implications of ethical issues regarding suicide.
3. Discuss the various meanings of self-destructive behavior.
4. Demonstrate skills in differential assessment of the acutely suicidal and chronically self-destructive person.
5. Plan strategies of crisis management and follow-up for self-destructive persons.
6. Discuss means for helping the survivors of suicide.
7. Identify social network and community resources for preventing unnecessary death.

PROGRAM CONTENT

1. Attitudes and feelings regarding suicide and self-destructive behavior.
2. Rights and responsibilities regarding self-destructive behavior.
3. Understanding the self-destructive person.
4. Principles and techniques of lethality assessment.
5. Crisis intervention with suicidal persons.
6. Comprehensive treatment and follow-up of self-destructive persons.
7. Helping survivors of suicide.
8. Community and social network approaches to suicide prevention.

METHODS

Workshop methods include faculty presentations, small group discussions, and faculty and participants' critique of group work sessions, with an emphasis on problem-solving techniques utilizing case examples from the participants' experience.

Continuing Education Workshop— Crisis Management for Victim Advocates

PRE-WORKSHOP QUESTIONNAIRE

Directions   Please review the attached draft of a crisis management workshop for victim advocates. To develop the proposed workshop to meet your continuing education needs as nearly as possible, we would appreciate your completion of the following questions. Return to: Massachusetts Office for Victim Assistance, 30 Winter St., Boston, MA 02108. Thank you.

Experience as a victim advocate:

_____ Less than 6 months

_____ 6 to 12 months

_____ 1 to 3 years

_____ more than 3 years

Experience in a related human service field: Specify type and length

of time_____

_____

_____

Training in crisis management/intervention: Specify (e.g., one-day

workshop, formal course in college, etc.)_____

_____

Training in a related human service field: Specify type and length of

time_____

_____

What do you hope to achieve from this workshop? Include any special issues or problems in the general topical area that you would like to have addressed.

Additional comments: (please use back of page)

DESCRIPTION

This one-day workshop includes the principles and techniques necessary for helping people in crisis. The focus is on the crisis management process applied to victims of crime. Problem solving through small group discussion and critique of case examples is emphasized.

OBJECTIVES

Participants will

1. Review crisis theory as a basis for understanding victims of crime.
2. Identify the steps of the crisis management process—Assessment, Planning, Implementation, and Evaluation.
3. Apply the crisis management process to the needs of various victims of crime served by victim advocates.
4. Explore the role of team relationships and interpersonal dynamics in assisting victims of crime.
5. Identify the indications and procedures for appropriate referral of victims with special needs for mental health service.

PROGRAM CONTENT

10:00   Review of crisis theory as it applies to victims of crime.

10:30   The crisis management process, basic steps—assessment, planning, implementation, and evaluation.

11:15   Break

11:30   Application to case examples identified by participants in small group discussion.

12:00   Critique and refinement of crisis management process based on case examples in a large group discussion.

12:45   Lunch

1:30   Critique and refinement and crisis management process (continued).

2:30   Team relationships and interpersonal dynamics.

3:00   Break

3:15   Criteria and procedures for mental health referrals.

3:45   Summary and evaluation.

Continuing Education Workshop— ▄▄▄▄▄▄▄▄▄▄
Violence in the Family: Prevention, Crisis Intervention, and Follow-Up

DESCRIPTION

Violence is a major problem in our society. Paradoxically, women, children, and the elderly are at the greatest risk in the family. Millions of family members are beaten or sexually abused each year. Additionally, many suffer double victimization by their treatment in health and criminal justice settings. What can you do to help victims and to stop the tide of violence in the United States?

This workshop will explore the problem of violence in the family in a sociocultural perspective. It is designed to assist health and other human service workers to understand, assess, and respond helpfully to victims of violence in community and hospital settings. The workshop is intended for nurses, physicians, and other staff of health and social service agencies. Group discussion and problem solving around case examples will be emphasized throughout.

OBJECTIVES

Workshop participants will:

1. Discuss facts in order to clarify myths, attitudes, and feelings regarding victims and perpetrators of violence.
2. Explore the social and cultural roots of violence in our society as a basis for prevention.
3. Explore principles and strategies to identify and assess victims of violence.
4. Discuss resources and approaches to assist victims during and following crisis from victimization.

PROGRAM CONTENT

1. Violence in the family: A national problem.
2. Social and cultural roots of violence.
3. Identification and assessment of actual and potential victims.
4. Identification of local resources for victim assistance.
5. Crisis intervention and follow-up service for victims.
6. Summary and evaluation.

Appendix C: Sample Training and Education Materials

Pre-Training Forms ▬▬▬▬▬▬▬▬▬▬▬▬▬▬▬
(from SPCS, Inc. of Tompkins County, Ithaca, NY)

Application Form. ▬▬▬▬▬▬▬▬▬▬▬▬

SUICIDE PREVENTION AND CRISIS SERVICE
of
Tompkins County, Inc.

Emergency phone — 272 - 1616   Business phone — 272 - 1505

Post Office Box 312   Ithaca, New York 14850

APPLICATION FOR SPCS TRAINING PROGRAM

Please fill out every item. Your answers will be completely confidential.
Return application to SPCS, Box 312, Ithaca, N.Y. 14850

Name_____

Address_____

Telephone (home)_____ (work)_____

Work hours_____ May you be contacted at work?_____

Date of birth_____ Number of children_____ Ages_____

Education: Name of school   Degree

    High school_____

    College_____

    Graduate School_____

    Professional/Technical training_____

    Coursework related to counseling_____

    _____

Employment status_____ Occupation_____

If employed outside the home, where_____

Previous employment:
            Employer   How long?

_____   _____

_____   _____

Volunteer activities (current and recent)
            Organization   How long?

_____   _____

_____   _____

How did you hear about Suicide Prevention and Crisis Service of Tompkins

County?_____

_____

Application - 2

Have you ever worked in a crisis intervention program before?_____

If yes, please describe (including a brief description of the training program):

_____

_____

Please list two personal references we may contact:

Name	Address & Telephone	Relationship
_____	_____	_____
_____	_____	_____

If your answer to any of the questions below is YES, this does not eliminate you from consideration. However, we would like you to discuss your participation in the SPCS training program during your interview in terms of the answers below.

Have you ever attempted suicide?   yes_____   No_____
Have you ever seriously considered
  suicide?   yes_____   No_____
Has anyone in your family committed
  suicide?   Yes_____   No_____
Have you ever been hospitalized for
  psychiatric reasons?   Yes_____   No_____
Have you ever called our service for help? Yes_____   No_____
Have you ever consulted a mental health
  professional about your own problems? Yes_____   No_____
If you are in psychotherapy, have you
  discussed taking this training
  with your therapist?   Yes_____   No_____

Briefly summarize your primary reasons for applying to this program.

_____

_____

_____

_____

What do you expect to get for yourself from this volunteer work?

_____

_____

_____

What do you think will be easiest for you?_____

_____

_____

Application - 3

What do you think will be the hardest for you?_____

_____

What doubts are in your mind as you prepare to enter the program?_____

_____

_____

What positive qualities do you have to offer to the program?_____

_____

_____

Please read carefully and sign at the time of your interview:

I agree not to see or visit any persons calling SPCS nor to communicate with them in any way except as authorized by the Center's staff.

I agree to commit myself to one year of service with SPCS.

I agree to fulfill my shift requirements of 15 hours a month, and attend both counselors and support group meetings.

I agree to comply with all the rules and regulations of Suicide Prevention and Crisis Service of Tompkins County, Inc. If accepted as a volunteer, I agree that all information I receive is confidential and is not to be discussed with anyone, including my spouse, close friends and/or relatives. I understand that any release of confidential information and/or direct personal contact made with any client of SPCS without consent of the staff will result in my release as a volunteer.

Date_____   Signed_____

_____

Shifts preferred: 8am - noon____   12pm - 5pm____
                    5pm - 10pm____   10pm - 8am____

Days preferred:

   Mon___   Tues___   Wed___   Thurs___   Fri___   Sat___   Sun___

Interest Inventory: Purpose - to make better use of the talents and interests of our volunteers.

___art   ___photography
___audio-visual equipment   ___professional skills (list)
___clerical skills   _____
___dramatics   ___public speaking
___editing   ___research
___fund raising   ___writing
___group leadership skills   ___writing press releases
___journalism   ___other_____
                                    _____
                                    _____

Interview checklist ▰▰▰▰▰▰▰▰▰▰▰▰▰▰

PERSONAL

1. What made you decide to get involved with SPCS at this time in your life?

2. Explore life experience: What difficult experiences has the person dealt with? How has she/he handled them? Check for stability, breadth of experience, coping, and maturity.

3. Religion: Would person describe self as religious? How does this impact on his/her thinking about abortion? About other issues with potential moral overtones (suicide, extra-marital sex, divorce, and gay/lesbian issues).

4. How would person describe this time in his/her life? (Watch for words like transition, from what to what? Is this a particularly stressful period? Are there major changes coming up in the very near future?)

5. Check out experience with therapy and attitudes about professional counseling.

6. Suicide: Use application as guideline for this discussion. If all answers on suicide questions are negative, ask if person has ever had *any* contact with suicide, fleeting thoughts, etc. If no, ask person what was the most difficult experience she/he has had, and how she/he coped with it.

7. Support system: Does person have a strong personal support network?

8. Emotional "soft spots": What kinds of issues, given either personal experience, belief system, or sheer inexperience, might make the person uncomfortable or judgmental and push personal buttons (cite such examples as a caller who won't take any personal responsibility—gay caller, battered women, child abuse situation, etc.). Ask person to discuss (see application questions, bottom p. 2, top p. 3).

INFORMATION

Describe other volunteer experience. Describe work situation (or school and future plans). How much does person know about SPCS? Provide information about kind of calls, shifts, and expectations for meetings, supervision, etc.

OBSERVATIONS

Watch for voice tone, expressiveness, use of language (does person express self well), intelligence (does person seem able to grasp basic concepts), comprehension of your questions, anxiety (how does person handle the interview situation), motivation (career goals, personal growth, way out of loneliness, back-door therapy, and getting to know community), sense of humor, perspective, eye contact, empathy, warmth, and in touch with own feelings.

ENDING THE INTERVIEW

Particularly for people about whom there are any questions, tell the individual that we are considering all the applications and will be in touch with him/her shortly to let him/her know about acceptance into the class.

Screening interview observations ▬▬▬▬▬▬▬

Name_____

Maturity and life experience:

Emotional stability:

Sense of humor:

Intelligence:

Openness:

Restrictions or limitations:

Stress coping:

Current situation:

Biases:

Special focus for training:

Comments: rating Interviewers:_____ − 1 2 3 4 +

_____− 1 2 3 4 +

Post Training Evaluation Forms ■■■■■■■■■■

Evaluation of SPCS Training Classes:

This questionaire must be filled out at the last session of the training. Your signature is optional.

1. How did you find out about the service?_____

_____

2. How did you feel about the application you were asked to complete?_____

_____

_____

3. What impressions did you carry away from your interview prior to training?

_____

_____

4. Did you feel the number of sessions provided enough initial training?

                 yes___   no___

5. Rate course trainer: Excellent___ Good___ Fair___ Poor___

6. Comment on the trainer's interaction with the class._____

_____

_____

_____

7. Rate handout material and information. Excellent___ Good___ Fair___
   Poor___

8. What did you like best in the packet?_____

9. What was least useful?_____

10. Rate overall course content. Excellent___ Good___ Fair___ Poor___

11. Which training session was most helpful to you?_____
    Why?_____

_____

12. Which session was least helpful to you?_____
    Why?_____

_____

13. Rate value of role playing to you in training sessions. Excellent___
    Good___ Fair___ Poor___ . Comments_____

_____

_____

Training evaluation - 2

14. What information would you prefer more detailed descriptions of?_____
_____
_____

15. For the coming monthly in-service meetings, suggest topics and/or speakers
to complement your present knowledge._____
_____
_____

16. Rate the participation of the training counselor in your training class.

Excellent___   Good___   Fair___   Poor___   Comments:_____
_____
_____

17. Are you comfortably familiar with:

    1. Applying the crisis intervention model? yes___   no___

    2. Office procedures?   yes___   no___

    3. How to find files you need?   yes___   no___

    4. Record keeping?   yes___   no___

    5. How to locate appropriate resources?   yes___   no___

    6. SPCS policies?   yes___   no___

    7. The consultative process?   yes___   no___

18. What further experience, after this final training session and your
apprentice shifts, would you prefer before handling a crisis call?
_____
_____
_____

19. How do you feel at the end of this training program as opposed to the way
you felt when you started the session?_____
_____
_____
_____

Comments, suggestions:_____
_____
_____
_____
_____
_____

Date_____   Signature(optional)_____

THREE MONTH FOLLOW-UP EVALUATION

Now that you have been working as a counselor for approximately three month, it would be helpful for us to have the following information.

1. How has your experience working for SPCS compared to your expectations?____

_____

_____

2. Did your training adequately prepare you to handle the kinds of calls you ha had to respond to? If not, what additional/different training might have been helpful?

Yes___ No___ Comment:_____

_____

_____

3. Do you find monthly counselor meetings useful? Yes___ No___ What would you like to see changed about these meetings?_____

_____

_____

4. Do you find your support group helpful? Yes___ No___ What would you like to see changed about your support group?_____

_____

_____

_____

5. What is there about SPCS office routine or policy that you would like to see changed?_____

_____

6. Do you feel integrated into the social community of SPCS?_____

_____

7. Have you called on a consultant (director, assistant, training counselor) durin any of your shifts? Yes___ No___ Was the response helpful? Please comment:

_____

_____

8. What would have made your apprentice shifts more helpful?_____

_____

9. Please make any comments that would be helpful to us in evaluating the effectiveness of training, the functioning of the office, etc. Use other side. Thank you for your assistance.

Role-Play Scenarios ▬▬▬▬▬▬▬▬▬▬▬▬▬▬▬▬▬

Role-plays for suicide session ▬▬▬▬▬▬▬▬▬▬▬▬▬

1. You are an elderly person. You live with your son and his family. You are interested in what your married children and grandchildren are doing, but it seems to you that none of them have any time for you. You feel as though you're in the way and of no use at all. You have begun to stay pretty much to yourself. You talk as though you want to die and be less trouble to those you love.

2. You are 16 years old. You say that people hassle you, especially your parents. You hint that you won't have to put up with it anymore. You have taken a mixture of 30–35 sleeping pills and barbiturates. You end up scared and wanting help.

3. A woman sounds as if she is between 30–35, but she will not identify herself. She asks what can the suicide prevention center do for a person who doesn't want to live anymore and generally takes a challenging position. The caller sounds controlled, makes vague allusions to a longstanding problem, and wants to know what you can do about it.

4. A man between 45–50 complains that his life is a mess because of his bungling. He talks about having gotten himself into such a jam financially, personally, or professionally that he feels the only way out is to kill himself. Often, he will be reacting to a specific recent setback in his life.

5. You are a college junior. You and your family have always wanted you to go to law school. Your grades have been slipping recently, and you just received a failing grade in a history final, sure to keep you out of law school. Your family has sacrificed a great deal to send you to school, and you can't bear to disappoint them. You'd rather be dead, so you're thinking of going somewhere and killing yourself.

6. A middle-aged women calls, complaining that she is very depressed, feels lonely and tired, and feels that no one is interested in her. She talks about many physical and medical problems. She says that she feels her doctor is not helping her enough, and her husband is not paying attention to her. She says she feels like her life is over, and there is no point in continuing to live.

Role-plays for session on
domestic violence

1. You're very nervous about making this call and want the counselor to guarantee your confidentiality. This is the first time you've ever talked to anyone about your situation, a physically abusive husband. It's been going on for the last two years and getting worse. He's a prominent person in town, and you are sure that no one will believe you. You are so desperate and frightened that you've been thinking of suicide. You're afraid to leave him—he's told you that he'll find you and kill you if you ever do.

2. You are the parent of a 3-year-old son who is driving you crazy. He's whining, demanding, and screams a lot. You feel like you're about to lose control. You did once, a month ago, you hurled him across the room, but fortunately he wasn't hurt badly. You feel it building up again; you're terrified of being reported for child abuse, but don't know where to turn.

3. You call after having been badly beaten by your husband last night. It's not the first time. It's happened several times in the past, usually when he's been drinking. You tried to leave him once, but without money and with two small children, you were desperate and frightened, so you went back. You'd like to get out now, but have no way to support yourself and the children. You're afraid to leave them with him because you might lose them in a custody fight if you walk out.

4. You came to the city to live with your boyfriend. You've only been here for two months and don't really know anyone but him. In the past few weeks he has become hostile and verbally abusive. You're growing frightened of him. He was divorced from a woman he admits to having beaten, but said it was because she was such a bitch. He has been threatening you. You don't know where to turn. You have no money of your own, no friends here, and your family is far away. Besides, they didn't want you to come here in the first place.

Approaches to High Risk Assessment

These scales are intended for use only in the context of thorough training in the clinical process and techniques of assessment for risk of suicide, homicide/assault, and victimization as described in *People in Crisis* (Hoff, 1984), Chapters 6 and 8. See appendix F for the community mental health record system from which these scales are excerpted.

Suicide risk assessment

KEY TO SCALE: DANGEROUSNESS TO SELF

1 =   *No predictable risk of suicide now.* No suicidal ideation or history of attempt, satisfactory social support system, and close contact with significant others.

2 =   *Low risk of suicide now.* Person has suicidal ideation with low lethal method, no history of attempts, or recent serious loss, and satisfactory support system.

3 =   *Moderate risk of suicide now.* Has suicidal ideation with high lethal method but no plan or threats. Has plan with low lethal method and history of low lethal attempts, e.g., employed female, age 35, divorced, with tumultuous family history.

4 =   *High risk of suicide now.* Has current high lethal plan with obtainable means, history of previous attempts, and no communication with a significant other, e.g., female, age 50, living alone, with drinking history, or black male, age 29, unemployed, and has lost his lover.

5 =   *Very high risk of suicide now.* Has current high lethal plan with available means, history of suicide attempts, and is removed, cut off from resources, e.g., white male, over 40, physically ill and depressed, wife threatening divorce, is unemployed, or has received promotion and fears failure.

LETHALITY ASSESSMENT EXERCISES

1. Assess selected case examples according to the above lethality assessment criteria and scales:

   Low Risk   Moderate Risk   High Risk
     1   2   3   4   5

2. Unable to assess—need more information. Specify *which* information and how it is to be obtained.

Assault/homicide risk assessment ▬▬▬▬▬▬▬

KEY TO SCALE: DANGEROUSNESS TO OTHERS

1 = *No predictable risk of assault or homicide now,* e.g., no homicidal ideation, urges, or history of same, basically satisfactory support system and social drinker only.

2 = *Low risk of homicide now,* e.g., has occasional assault or homicidal ideation with some urges to kill, no history of impulsive acting out or homicidal attempts, occasional drinking bouts, and basically satisfactory social support system.

3 = *Moderate risk of homicide now,* e.g., has frequent homicidal ideation and urges to kill, but no specific plan, history of impuslive acting out, but no homicide attempts, episodic drinking bouts, and stormy relationships with significant other with periodic high tension arguments.

4 = *High risk of homicide now,* e.g., has homicidal plan with obtainable means, drinking history, history of impulsive acting out, but no homicide attempts, stormy relationships, and much verbal plus occasional physical fighting with significant others.

5 = *Very high risk of homicide now,* e.g., has current high lethal plan with available means, history of homicide attempts or impulsive acting out, feels a strong urge to "get even" with a significant other, and history of drinking with possibly also high lethal suicide risk.

LETHALITY ASSESSMENT EXERCISES

1. Assess selected case examples according to the above lethality assessment criteria and scales:

Low Risk		Moderate Risk		High Risk
1	2	3	4	5

2. Unable to assess—need more information. Specify *which* information and how it is to be obtained.

Victimization assessment ▬▬▬▬▬▬▬

KEY TO SCALE: EXPERIENCE AND TRAUMA OF VIOLENCE

1 = *No experience of physical violence.* No memory of violence recently or in the past. Very stable support network.

2 = *Experience of violence with minor physical and/or emotional trauma.*
Currently, verbal arguments with family or intimates which occasionally escalate to pushing, shoving, or mild slapping. Stable support network. History may include occasional mild physical discipline as a child, one past incident of sexual abuse (e.g., fondling) by
a non-family member when under age five, and physical struggle
with a stranger during purse snatching.

3 = *Experience of violence with moderate physical and/or emotional trauma.*
Physically abused by family member or intimate several times a
month during past two years resulting in mild physical injury, e.g.,
bruises, no threat to life, and no guns available. Unresponsive
support network. History may include one incident of sexual abuse
(e.g., fondling) by a parent or step-parent over two years ago, rape
by a stranger over two years ago, moderate physical injury during
purse snatching, and informal counseling for past victimization.

4 = *Experience of violence with severe physical and/or emotional trauma.*
Physically abused by family member or intimate several times a
month during past two years resulting in serious physical injury,
e.g., requiring medical treatment with threats to kill but no guns
available. Very unresponsive support network. History may include
frequent sexual abuse (e.g., including intercourse) by a parent or
step-parent in the past and currently, raped by a stranger, acquain-
tance, or intimate within past six months, other physical attack by a
stranger requiring medical treatment but no permanent scars, and
no counseling for past victimization.

5 = *Life-threatening or prolonged violence with very severe physical and/or
emotional trauma.* Recent (past three months) or current life-threatening physical abuse and guns available. Socially, very isolated. No
counseling or support around past or present abuse and victimization. History may include severe abuse requiring medical treatment
in past two years, routine sexual abuse (including intercourse) by a
parent or step-parent now and in the past, recent rape at gun or
knifepoint, and other physical attack by a stranger requiring extensive medical treatment and leaving permanent physical scars.

Appendix D: Sample Table of Contents for Crisis Staff Manual

CONTENTS

Team conference
Clinical conference
Consultation conference
Secretarial-receptionist

Quality Control and Evaluation
Intra-staff consultation and team (peer) relationships
Staff supervisory program
Extra-staff consultation
Peer utilization review committee
Client grievance process
Objective evaluation program

Public Relation Community Education Program

Agency Staff
Employment
Promotion
Staff development program
Intra-unit
Extra-unit, meetings, etc.
Staff evaluation

Volunteer and Students
Volunteer program
Student field placements

APPENDIX

Structure and organization
Organization chart
Staff members and unit heads—summary of staff qualifications
Citizen board members
Street directory and catchment area maps

Direct service forms
Record samples
Fee cards
Referral forms

Indirect service
Consultee agencies
Consultation forms

Conference and meeting schedules

Peer utilization review procedure

Current public relations contacts

Agency personnel policies
  Job specifications
  Personnel practices committee policy and procedure

Volunteer Data Forms

CMHC Policy Regarding Student Field Placement

Staff In-service and Education Materials

Appendix E: Sample Code of Ethics for a Crisis Service

American Association of Suicidology
Guidelines for a Code of Ethics for Suicide Prevention
and Crisis Intervention

I. Purpose

To establish guidelines for a code of ethics for individual and center members of the American Association of Suicidology (AAS) involved with prevention or crisis intervention (hereinafter referred to as crisis workers).

II. Objectives

1. To protect the rights of persons provided services by, or participating in programs of, members of AAS.
2. To promote compliance with professional and community standards of conduct.
3. To provide guidelines for the resolution of ethical conflicts in suicide prevention and crisis intervention procedures.

III. Principles

1. Integrity

    a. The crisis worker shall place the highest value on integrity. Whether as a practitioner, teacher, trainer, or researcher, there should be no compromise with the best interests of the persons served being the overriding consideration at all times.

2. Competence

    a. Responsibility should only be undertaken or assigned for those activities for which the person has been trained and has demonstrated an adequate level of competence. If the needs of the person being helped are beyond the competence of the crisis worker, referral to someone with the needed skills should be accomplished as expeditiously as possible, assuring that possible feelings of rejection or abandonment are appropriately dealt with.

    b. If lack of competence is observed in other persons or agencies, the observation should be made known to one's supervisor or to the individual responsible for taking corrective action.

c. If physical or emotional problems interfere with the crisis worker's optimal functioning, appropriate steps should be taken to see that such problems do not compromise the quality of services offered. The interests of the person being helped are first dealt with, and measures to correct the crisis worker's problems instituted as well. Further crisis work should be deferred until such problems no longer interfere with the person's competence.

3. Moral Standards

a. The crisis worker should respect the social and moral attitudes of the community in which he/she works, assuring that the reputation of persons or agencies not be unnecessarily jeopardized.

4. Legal Standards

a. In the course of crisis work, illegal actions by the person in crisis should not be encouraged or facilitated. If a legal issue is present, of which the person being helped is not aware, the crisis worker should inform the person of that issue. In no case should the crisis worker participate in an illegal act.

5. Representation

a. The crisis worker shall accurately represent his/her qualifications, affiliations and purposes when appropriate, and those of the agency with which he/she is associated.

b. The crisis worker should not provide information which would imply the presence of qualifications or affiliations, professional or otherwise, that are not accurate, or would lead others to assume qualities or characteristics that are not correct. If misrepresented by others, or if incorrect assumptions are made by others, the crisis worker should rectify such misconceptions.

c. The crisis worker should not use his/her affiliation with an organization, or its divisions, for purposes which are not consonant with the stated purpose of that organization.

6. Public Statements

a. All public statements, whether direct or indirect, should be accurate and free of sensationalism, bias, distortion or misrepresentation of any kind. Special care in this regard is required in activities related to news articles aimed at stimulating public awareness and support of an agency, and for solicitation of funds to continue the agency's work.

b. When information is provided to the public about suicide prevention or crisis intervention techniques, it should be made clear that such techniques are to be used only by persons adequately trained in their use, when that is the case.

c. In any communication with the public, care should be taken to avoid implication that the crisis worker or agency endorses the purchase or use of a commercial product or service.

7. Confidentiality

a. Maintaining the confidentiality of information about persons helped is a primary responsibility. Such information should not be communicated to others unless specific provisions for such release are met.

b. Confidential information may be revealed after careful consideration indicates the presence of clear and present danger to an individual or to society, and then only to those who must be informed in order to reduce that danger.

c. Information about persons being helped may be discussed only with others clearly concerned with the case, and then strictly for professional purposes.

d. Except for b. and c. above, only when the person being helped gives express permission may information be disclosed to another individual. The person should specify what information may be given, and to whom.

e. Written and oral reports should contain only information germane to the purpose of the report. Every effort should be made to protect the person's privacy.

f. In writing and teaching, care should be taken that any clinical material used should be presented in such a way that the identity of the individual is not revealed.

g. The identity of research subjects should not be revealed or rendered recognizable without explicit permission.

h. The crisis worker should assure that appropriate provisions are made for the maintenance of confidentiality in the storage, retrieval, use and ultimate disposition of records.

8. Welfare of Persons Receiving Crisis Services

a. In accord with 2.a above, if it becomes clear that the person the crisis worker is responding to would be best served by referral to another crisis worker, or another type of assistance, such referral should be accomplished without undue delay. Full consideration should be given to the possible adverse effects of referral, and the procedure carried out in such a manner that these potential adverse effects are minimized.

b. In the event of referral, the referring crisis worker should continue to render assistance as needed, until such time as the responsibility for helping the person is assumed fully, if that is appropriate, by the worker taking over the case.

9. Relationship with the Person Receiving Crisis Service
   a. Crisis services should be provided only in the context of a professional type of program.
   b. No illegal interaction should transpire in the course of providing crisis services.
   c. The crisis worker should not provide services to his/her associates, friends, or family members except in the most unusual circumstances, and then only with the concurrence of an experienced consultant.
   d. Each individual agency should state, in its policies and procedures manual, precisely under which circumstances a call may be taped or listened to by a third party without the caller's knowledge or consent. An opinion on this issue should be obtained from legal counsel that relevant federal or state laws would not be violated by these policies and procedures.

10. Offering of Services
    a. Any proffering of suicide prevention and crisis services should be carried out within strict limits of community standards, propriety and good taste.
    b. Notices designed for public use, such as telephone book, posters, or brochures, may contain a statement of the name, degree, certification and sponsoring agency of the provider, the services offered, a description of those services, circumstances in which the services might appropriately be used, and how to obtain them. Reassurances, such as emphasizing twenty-four hour readiness to respond, and desire to be of help, may be included in material from agencies or organizations.
    c. No evaluative statements or assurance of quality or efficacy should be expressed or implied in any form.

11. Professional Relations
    a. The integrity, traditions and potential helping role of all professions and disciplines should be acknowledged and respected, both in relations between disciplines and in communications with persons in crisis. No suggestion of precedence among disciplines should be expressed or implied, though special needs may call for unique skills in individual cases.
    b. Crisis workers should not knowingly enter into a competitive role with other providers in the community. If the person being helped has a previously established relationship with another caregiver, the crisis worker should attempt to integrate the efforts being made. In no case should there be an effort to prevent the other caregiver from being informed of the crisis worker's role. Mutual agreement of all concerned, as to the best way to assist the person in crisis, should be striven for.

12. Remuneration
    a. No commission, rebate or other consideration or inducement should be involved in a referral to or from a crisis worker for the provision of crisis services.
    b. The crisis worker should not use his/her relationship with the person being helped to promote his/her own benefit or that of any agency or of any other enterprise.
    c. A crisis worker associated with an agency or institution should not accept a fee or other form of remuneration for providing services to a person who is entitled to those services through the agency or institution.
    d. A crisis worker in an agency or institution should not accept a gift from a person being helped, unless its nature and value falls within the limits established by the governing body of the agency or institution for such gifts.

13. Ownership of Materials
    a. All materials prepared by a crisis worker, in carrying out his/her regular duties in an organization, shall be the property of that organization. Release or publication of such materials will be governed by the policies established by the organization.
    b. Materials prepared by a crisis worker in an agency, other than those materials resulting from his/her regular duties, shall, if published, and the agency so desires, include a

disclaimer of responsibility on the part of the agency for the content of the published materials.

14. Promotional Activities
    a. A crisis worker or agency associated with the promotion of services, books, or other products, should ensure that these are presented in a professional and factual manner.
    b. Any claims made should be supported by scientifically acceptable evidence.
    c. If a financial interest is held in any commercial product, care must be taken to assure that the clinical care of persons in crisis is not adversely affected by that interest.
15. Research
    a. All research activity must be carried out with meticulous attention to the well-being and dignity of all participants.
    b. The design and methodology of clinical studies shall follow federal guidelines for research involving human subjects.
    c. Research carried out in an agency or institution must be reviewed and approved by the governing board of that institution, which must determine that compliance with human rights regulations will be observed.

pendix F: Sample Clinical Record Systems

Community Mental Health Center ▬▬▬▬▬▬▬▬▬▬

The Community Mental Health record system is reprinted with permission of the Erie County Mental Health Department, Buffalo, NY and Addison-Wesley Publishing Company. Readers are referred to *People in Crisis* (Hoff, 1984a), pp. 91 and 92 for a full description of these forms and directions to obtain complete specifications for their use.

Community Mental Health Record System ■■■■■

Today's Date _1-15-84_
Time _5:30_ AM
(PM)

Walk-in _____
Phone _____
Outreach _Police_
Written _____

ID # _101_
SS # _123-98-456_
Welfare/
Medicaid # _____

SERVICE REQUESTED FOR
Client's NAME _____George_____O._____||_____Sloan_____
              First   Middle   Last

                                                      Permanent _✔_
Address __33 Random Avenue___Middletown___01234___Central___Temporary_____
         Street   City/Town   Zip   County   Catchment Area _3_

Phone # _123-0987_ Means of Transportation _Ambulance_
Directions to home _____
(if outreach)
Sex __Male _✔_   Date of Birth _1936_____Age _48_
   Female ____

SERVICE REQUESTED BY
□ AGENCY   Name _____ Phone #_____
□ OTHER   Address _____ Time(s) seen by
□ SELF   If Agency- Contact Person _____ the agency_____

PRESENTING SITUATION/PROBLEM - What made you decide to seek help today?
(use other side if needed)

George Sloan, 48, was brought to E.R. by police following a
suicide attempt by car crash. His intention was to die as he
saw no way out of his personal and family problems. Has
had heart trouble for 4 years. Was urged to quit second job and take
office job in Police Dept. His 16-yr. old son's suspension from school
adds to his sense of failure. Feels he has no one to talk to. Had
considered suicide after last heart attack but support from his
his wife prevented him then from crashing his car. While initially
reluctant, Mr. Sloan now seems open to counseling assistance.

Have you talked with anyone about this? Yes ____ Who? _____
Address _____ No _✔_   Phone # _____
                        Date of last contact- _____
Are you taking ANY medication now?   Yes _✔_   What? 1. _nitroglycerine_
(If more than 3 begin list on MH-2)No _____
                                                    2. _____

CRISIS RATING How urgent is your need for help?
🗶 Immediate (within minutes)   3. _____
□ Within a few hours
□ Within 24 hours
□ Within a few days
□ Within a week or two

Comments
Recommend Mr. Sloan receive full assessment and crisis counseling while being treated for injuries from suicidal car accident, plus follow-up with entire family.

DISPOSITION (Check all that apply)
🗶 Crisis
🗶 Medical Emergency
🗶 Assessment (specify)- _Individual and Family_
□ Discharge Planning
□ Expediting/Advocacy
□ Other (explain)- _____
🗶 Referral made to- _Psychiatric Liason Service_   Confirmed—Yes _✔_No___ Date _1-15-84_
Date of Next Contract_____ Assigned to _John Doe, MSW_
Date of Assignment _____ Request taken by _Jane Doe, RN_

MH-1

COMPREHENSIVE MENTAL HEALTH ASSESSMENT

ID # _____

Name _____
First   Middle   Last

Assessment Date _____ Time _____ AM / PM   Place of Assessment _____

RATING SCALE

1	2	3	4	5
High Functioning	High/Moderate Functioning	Moderate Functioning	Low/Moderate Functioning	Low Functioning

(W = Worker; C = Client; O = Other)

A. LIFE FUNCTIONS

1. Physical Health   -Medical Information (Include relevant items; eg. illnesses, surgery, physical impairment, allergies, pregnancy, birth defects)

Current medical care   Yes ___ No ___
Family Physician or Medical Clinic(s) NAME _____
Address _____ Last time seen _____
Phone _____

Medication Use	Name	Dosage	Duration	Physician/Clinic
1.				
2.				
3.				
4.				
5.				

Comments:

W   C   O
__ __ __

2. Self-Acceptance/Self-Esteem

Comments:

W   C   O
__ __ __

3. Vocational/Occupational ___ Employed ___ Homemaker ___ Student ___ Other ___
Employer/School
Name _____ Job Title (Functional) _____
Address _____ How long? _____
Phone # _____ Unemployed _____ How long? _____
(Optional) Education/Training _____

Comments:

W   C   O
__ __ __

4. Immediate Family   Parental Status-

      Children? Yes___No___How many? _____

Comments:

	W	C	O
	__	__	__

(Refer to Child Screening Checklist if appropriate)

5. Intimate Relationships   Martial Status-

Never
Married_____ Married_____ Widowed____ Divorced_____ Separated___Together_____ Long ____

    Comments:

	W	C	O
	__	__	__

6. Residential   Living situation-

Lives alone___Lives with family___Other___(specify)_____

Comments:

	W	C	O
	__	__	__

SIGNIFICANT OTHER INFORMATION

Name	Nature of Relationship	Age	Grade *	Within Household	Outside Household Address	Phone

*Special Class Placement

MH-2A

COMPREHENSIVE MENTAL HEALTH ASSESSMENT (con't.)

Name _____   ID# _____

7. Financial   Source of income _____
   Comments:

                                                        W   C   O
                                                        —   —   —

8. Decision Making/Cognitive Functions
   Comments:

                                                        W   C   O
                                                        —   —   —

9. Life Philosophy/Goals
   What are your life goals?   i. _____
                                      2. _____
   Comments: 3. _____

                                                        W   C   O
                                                        —   —   —

10. Leisure Time/Community Involvement
    Comments:

                                                        W   C   O
                                                        —   —   —

11. Feeling Management
    Comments:

                                                        W   C   O
                                                        —   —   —

MH-3

RATING SCALE

1	2	3	4	5
High Functioning	High/Moderate Functioning	Moderate Functioning	Low/Moderate Functioning	Low Functioning

B. SIGNALS OF DISTRESS

12. <u>Violence Experienced</u>   History of Attacks and Injury

Date(s)_____

____within last month
____within last 6 months
____within last year
____over 1 year

<u>Outcomes</u>

____ Medical treatment only
____ Shelter
____ Referral (social service or marital counseling)
____ Referral (psychiatry)
____ No medical or other service
____ Other

Describe attack (beating, rape, etc.):

Total number of attacks _____ Date of last attack _____

Comments (include context, injury, aftermath):

	W	C	O
	—	—	—

13. <u>Lethality-Self</u>   History of Self-Injury-

Date _____ Method _____   Outcome_____

____ within last month
____ within last 6 months
____ within last year
____ over 1 year ago

____ Medical Treatment Only
____ Hosp. Intensive Care
____ Hosp. Psychiatric
____ Out-pt. Follow-up
____ No Treatment

Total number of suicide attempts _____ Date of last attempt _____

Comments: (include ideation and threats)

	W	C	O
	—	—	—

14. <u>Lethality-Other</u>

History of Injury to Other

Date(s)_____ Method-

____within last month
____within last 6 months
____within last year
____over 1 year

Total number of assaults___ _____ Date of last assault _____

<u>Client</u>   <u>Outcome</u>   <u>Other</u>

____Medical Treatment Only   ____
____Hosp. Intensive Care   ____
____Hosp. Psychiatric   ____
____Out-pt. Follow-Up   ____
____No Treatment   ____

Comments: (include ideation and threats)

	W	C	O
	—	—	—

15. <u>Substance Use</u>-Drug and/or Alcohol
Other Drug Use (include alcohol use)

	Type	Present Use	Past Use	Duration
1.				
2.				
3.				
4.				
5.				
6.				

Comments:

	W	C	O
	—	—	—

COMPREHENSIVE MENTAL HEALTH ASSESSMENT (cont.)

Name _____ ID# _____

16. Legal

   a. Pending Court Action   Yes ____   No ____   When _____

   b. On Probation   Yes ____   No ____   Probation Officer _____

   c. On Parole   Yes ____   No ____   Parole Officer _____

   d. Conditional Discharge   Yes ____   No ____

Comments:

                                         W   C   O

                                         —   —   —

17. Agency Use

Previous Mental Health Service Contacts

   Outcare: Name of Agency _____ Phone # _____

            Contact Person _____ Date of last Contact _____

            Address _____

   Incare: Name of Agency _____ Phone # _____

          Contact Person _____

          Address _____ Date of last Hosp. _____

          Reason for Admission _____

          How often _____ How long _____ Avg. length of stay _____

Comments:

                                         W   C   O

                                         —   —   —

Optional Information

   Religious Concerns ___ Yes ___ No ___ What _____

   Ethnic Cultural Background Problems Yes ___ No ___ What _____

Narrative Summary of Assessment:

Assessed by _____ Date _____ MH-4

COMPREHENSIVE MENTAL HEALTH ASSESSMENT

Client Self-Assessment Worksheet

Date _1-15-84_ Name _George Sloan_

Circle one for each question.

1. Physical Health

   How is your health?

   Comments: _No problems except for heart._
   Feel OK except for chest pain, which is getting
   more frequent.

   Excellent
   Good
   (Fair)
   Poor
   Very Poor

2. Self-Acceptance/Self-Esteem

   How do you fell about yourself as a person?

   Comments: _Not very good - especially when I think_
   about my son's trouble that it's probably my
   fault. Seems like I'm no good at anything
   lately.

   Excellent
   Good
   Fair
   (Poor)
   Very Poor

3. Vocational/Occupational

   (Includes student & homemaker)
   How would you judge your work/school situation?

   Comments: _I can still do patrol work but the_
   doctor says I should slow down.

   Excellent
   Good
   (Fair)
   Poor
   Very Poor

4. Immediate Family

   How are your relationships with your family and/or spouse?

   Comments: _Ever since my first heart attack_
   we seem to be going from bad to worse,
   especially with our son Arnold.

   Excellent
   Good
   Fair
   (Poor)
   Very Poor

5. Intimate Relationship(s)

   Is there anyone you feel really close to and can rely on?

   Comments: _Not really. Things used to be better_
   between my wife and me, but we seem
   to be drifting apart.

   Always
   Usually
   Sometimes
   (Rarely)
   Never

6. Residential

   How do you judge your housing situation?

   Comments: _____

   (Excellent)
   Good
   Fair
   Poor
   Very Poor

7. Financial

   How would you describe your financial situation?

   Comments: _As long as I have my second job_
   it's OK, but I don't like the idea of my
   wife working full time.

   Excellent
   (Good)
   Fair
   Poor
   Very Poor

8. Decision Making ability

   How satisfied are you with your ability to make life decisions?

   Comments: _Mostly around the problems we_
   have with Arnold.

   Always Very Satisfied
   Almost Always Satisfied
   (Occasionally Dissatisfied)
   Almost Always Dissatisfied
   Always Very Dissatisfied

9. Life Philosophy/Goals

Circle one for each question.

How satisfied are you with how your life goals are working for you?

Comments: *I almost always felt satisfied before the heart trouble started 4 years ago.*

Always Very Satisfied
Almost Always Satisfied
Occasionally Dissatified
(Almost Always Dissatisfied)
Always Very Dissatisfied

10. Leisure Time/Community Involvement

How satisfied are you with your use of free time?

Comments: *I don't have much free time, but I really like my work. I suppose our whole family could use more time together*

Always Very Satisfied
Almost Always Satisfied
(Occasionally Dissatisfied)
Almost Always Dissatisfied
Always Very Dissatisfied

11. Feeling Management

How comfortable are you with your feelings?

Comments: *Just during the last few months I really started feeling depressed. My wife says I bottle everything up.*

Always Very Comfortable
Almost Always Comfortable
(Occasionally Uncomfortable)
Almost Always Uncomfortable
Always Very Uncomfortable

12. Violence Experienced

To what extent have you been troubled by physical violence against you?

Comments: _____

(Never)
Once only
Several times within 6 months
Once or twice a month
Routinely (every day or so)

13. Lethality (self)

Is there any current risk of suicide for you?

Comments: *I still can't see any way out except suicide, but right now I feel a little better from talking with you.*

No Predictable Risk of Suicide Now
Low Risk of Suicide Now
Moderate Risk of Suicide Now
High Rsik of Suicide Now
(Very High Risk of Suicide Now)

14. Lethality (other)

Is there any risk that you might physically harm someone?

Comments: _____

(No Predictable Risk of Assult Now)
Low Risk of Assault Now
Moderate Risk of Assault Now
High Risk of Assault Now
Very High Risk of Assault Now

15. Substance Use (Drug and/or Alcohol)

Does use of drugs/alcohol interfere with performing your responsiblities?

Comments: _____

(Never Interferes)
Rarely Interferes
Sometimes Interferes
Frequently Intereferes
Constantly Interferes

16. Legal

What is your tendency to get in trouble with the law?

Comments: _____

(No Tendency)
Slight Tendency
Moderate Tendency
Great Tendency
Very Great Tendency

17. Agency Use

How successful are you with at getting help from agencies (or doctors) when you need it?

Comments: *I don't like going to doctor's and avoid it if at all possible.*

Always Successful
(Usually Successful)
Moderately Successful
Seldom Successful
Never Successful

Any additional comments?

MH-6A

Child Screening Checklist

ID#_____

Child's Full Name_____Sex____Birthdate_____

School Problems
a) poor grades___   d) suspended___
b) does not get along with students___   e) poor attendance___
c) does not get along with teachers___

Family Relationship Problems
does not get along with: father___ mother___ brothers___ sisters___
refuses to participate in family activities___
refuses to accept and perform family responsibilities___

Peer Relationship Problems
prefers to be alone___   prefers to be with adults___
does not associate with age mates___   not accepted by others___

Dyssocial Behavior
excessive lying___ hurts others___ hurts self___ destructive___ runaway___
substance use___ court involvement___ other___

Personal Adjustment Problems
temper tantrums___ easily upset___ speech problems___ sleep disturbances___
nervous mannerisms___ eating problems___ fearful___ lacks self-confidence___
clinging and dependent___ wetting, soiling, retention___ other___

Medical and Developmental Problems
chronic illness___ allergies___ physical handicaps___ accident prone___
seizures___ physical complaints___ lengthy or frequent hospitalizations___
medication___ surgery___ MR___ other___

Development Milestones (Administer to all pre-schoolers. Check behaviors present, up to and including present age.)

Age	Activity	Age	Activity
1	____ imitates speech sounds	2 1/2	____ climbs stairs,
1	____ feeds self with fingers		alternating feet
1	____ pulls self to feet	3	____ forms sentences
1 1/2	____ uses single words	3	____ dresses self--no fasteners
1 1/2	____ walks alone	4	____ recognizes three colors
2	____ understands simple directions	4	____ throws ball overhand
2	____ scribbles with pencil or crayon	5	____ speaks clearly
2 1/2	____ combines words into phrases	5	____ buttons clothing

In years or months, at what age do you think your child is functioning _____

Strengths and assets:

Comments:

Screened by _____ Date _____

SERVICE CONTRACT   S=Satisfied   U=Unsatisfied

Name _____ ID# _____

Significant Other _____

Case Manager _____

Back up _____

Code

1. Physical
2. Self-Acceptance
3. Vocational
4. Immediate Family
5. Intimate Relationship(s)
6. Residential
7. Financial
8. Decision Making
9. Life Philosophy
10. Leisure Time/ Community Involvement
11. Feeling Management
12. Lethality (self)
13. Lethality (other)
14. Substance Use
15. Legal
16. Agency Use
17. Violence Experienced.

Code #	Date	Problem Statement	Method/Technique/Tasks for achieved goals (include review date)	Expected Outcome (include date)	Goal Achieved S or U	Date

MH-7

ORIGINAL CALL SHEET

PHONE Name and No._____   Caller Name_____
                                       Address_____
Date_____   Phone No._____
    M   T   W   Th   F   Sa   Su   Referred by_____

Time:_____Began_____Term am-pm   3rd Party: Name_____
                                                    Phone_____
Length:_____Hours_____mins.   Relation to Caller_____
PHONE Line: 00   10   81
Log Page Number_____   Zip Code_____

Counseling Agency:_____Therapist:_____

Caller:

Age_____R/G Sex: M   F   Race_____Marital Status_____Student_____
Occupation_____Living Situation_____
Affect, Behavior, Special Identifying Characteristics:_____

_____ _____

_____

Lethality_____Probability of Attempt_____DNA____
(See attached Assessment Sheet_____)

I. Establishing Rapport (What feelings were explored?)

II. Exploring Content and Feelings

III. Focus (Usually a feeling associated with the P.E.)

IV. **Exploring** Choices (tuning in is important here)

   1. Callers: (a) Past coping attempts:

      (b) Other ideas:

   2. Yours:

V. **Plan of Action** 'Be Specific: include referrals if made'

VI. **Counselor's Impressions and Feelings**

                  Was Back-Up consulted?___Yes___No
                  Was a follow-up arranged?___Yes___No
                  - Purpose of FU/points to cover_____

                  Outcalls made in connection with this call_____

Staff Feedback

BATON ROUGE CRISIS INTERVENTION CENTER, INC.   4/85

SUICIDE ASSESSMENT SHEET

PHONE Name & No. _____ Date_____ Caller_____

I. First, complete the work sheet on the reverse side for lethality and probability of attempt variables. Using the completed work sheet, your experience, and your judgement, assess both lethality and probability of attempt below (Please circle)

     LETHALITY   LOW   MEDIUM   HIGH   PROBABILITY OF ATTEMPT LOW   MEDIUM   HIGH

II. Describe Present Plan (include suicidal statements and clues):

III. Previous Suicide Attempts:

    Dates: Method: Outcome:

IV. Significant others (relatives, friends, therapists, helping agencies):

    Name: Relationship: Address: Phone No. Present Communication

V. Survivor's History (significant others who have suicided)

    Who_____

    When _____

    Caller's response _____

VI. Ambivalence: Did the caller acknowledge ambivalence?_____

                 Living Clues: Dying Clues

VIII. Plan of Action:

    _____Own resources (specify) ———————————Outreach Team:

    _____ To Live Decision   ——————————— Consulted

    _____ Dispose of means   ——————————— Implemented

    _____ Eat, sleep, etc.   ——————————— Emergency Procedures:

    _____ Recontact THE PHONE ——————————— Ambulance/ Police sent

    _____External Resources:

    _____ Counseling

    _____ Contact Significant
                          Others

    _____Follow-Up Call

CHECK FOR " SUICIDE IN PROGRESS" ____

LETHALITY	LOW	MEDIUM	HIGH
1. SUICIDE PLAN (describe on reverse) Method	__pills, slash wrist	__drugs & alcohol, car wreck	__gun, hanging, jumping
Chance of intervention	__others present	__others available or expected	__no one nearby, isolated

PROBABILITY OF ATTEMPT	LOW	MEDIUM	HIGH
1. SUICIDE PLAN (describe on reverse) Details	__vague, no plan	__some specifics	__very specific, knows how, when, where
Time	__no specific time or in the future	__within a few hours	__immediately, or in progress
Availability of means	__not available, will have to get	__available, have close by	__have in hand or in progress
2. PREVIOUS SUICIDE ATTEMPTS (describe on reverse) Number / Lethality	__none or one of low lethality	__multiple of low lethality or one of moderate lethality, history of repeated threats	__one high to multiple attempts of moderate lethality
When	__over two years ago	__six months to two years	__within last six months
3. INTERNAL RESOURCES Affect Anxiety	__mild, some discomfort is felt	__moderate, discomfort is increasing but not overwhelming	__high, feels overwhelmed, may panic
Depression	__mild, feels slightly down	__moderate, increased feelings of sadness & hopelessness with a decrease of energy	__severe, overwhelming feelings of sadness & hopelessness with a marked energy decrease
Coping Behavior Daily functioning	__daily activities continue as usual with little change	__some daily activities are set aside, some disturbance in eating, sleeping, & work habits	__many daily activities are discontinued-gross disturbances in eating, sleeping, & work habits
Stress reaction	__no significant stress	__moderate reaction to loss, sickness, and other environmental changes	__severe reaction to loss, sickness, and other environmental changes
Present coping strategies	__generally constructive, utilizing resources, verbalizing feelings	__some that are constructive, others that are maladaptive, increased drinking	__predominantly maladaptive, excessive drinking, drug usage, risk taking behavior
4. EXTERNAL RESOURCES (as perceived by caller-describe on reverse) Availability	__help available, sign. others concerned and willing to help	__family & friends available but unwilling to consistently help, esp. financially	__family, therapist, clergy, employer, hostile, exhausted or injurious to caller
Communication	__frequent positive interaction with more than one sign. other	__positive interaction w/ at least 1 sign. other	__little and/or poor interaction w/ sign. others
5. MEDICAL STATUS	__no significant medical problems	__acute (short term) psychosomatic illness (asthma, ulcers, muscle cramps, hyperventilation, etc.)	__chronic (long term) debilitating illness, or acute catastrophic illness (cancer, rabies, etc.)
6. LIFE STYLE HISTORY	__fairly consistent work history, stable relationships, stable personality, no history of violent behavior	__crisis in stable personality, recent increase in long standing, disabling personality traits, some violence noted in past behavior, alcoholism, drug addiction, homosexuality	__chronic suicidal behavior in unstable personality, recurrent outbreak of severe symptoms, difficulty in peer, family, and job relationships, repeated violent outbursts

*SAS from Suicide Prevention Center of Dallas, Inc. and Suicide Assessment and Intervention by Hatton, Valente, and Rink were used as resources for developing this form.
BRCIC, INC.   11/80

Revised 11/85

LETHALITY ASSESSMENT

FACTOR	LOW	MEDIUM	HIGH
1. Suicide plan -method	pills, knife, razor	drugs & alcohol,	guns, hanging, carbon monoxide, poisoning, jumping
-details	vague, no plans	some specifics	very specific- knows how, when, where
-time	no specific time, sometime in future	within a few hrs.	immediately, or in progress
-availability of means	not available, will have to obtain	available, have close by	in hand, or in-progress
-chance of intervention	others present	others available or close by	no one nearby, isolated
2. Previous suicide attempts: number/ lethality	none, or one of low lethality	multiple of low lethality, or one of moderate leth. history of repeated threats.	multiple attempts of moderate lethality, or one of high lethality.
-when	over 2 yrs. ago	6 months to 2 yrs.	within last 6 months
3. Internal resources -affect, anxiety	mild, some discomfort felt	moderate, discomfort increasing but not overwhelming	high, feels overwhelmed
-ambivalence	gives off living clues, life still matters	questions own life, living clues still may be present	has put affairs in order--ready to die, no future oriented plans
-depression	mild, feels slightly down	moderate, increased feelings of sadness	severe, overwhelming feelings of sadness
-hostility	little or none	some irritation, annoyance	resentful, discontent, marked anger
-coping behavior (daily functioning)	continues as usual with little change	some daily activities are set aside, some disturbances in eating, sleeping and work habits	many daily activities are discontinued, gross disturbances in eating, sleeping & work habits
-stress reaction	no significant stress	a moderate reaction to loss, sickness & other enviromental changes	a severe reaction to loss, sickness or other enviromental changes
-present coping strategies	generally construtive, utilizing resources, verbalizing feelings, (mild experimentation w/ substances)	somewhat construc-tive, maladaptive increased drinking and/or drug use	predominantly maladaptive, excessive drinking or drug use, risk-taking behavior present

FACTOR	LOW	MODERATE	HIGH
4. External resources (as perceived by caller) -availability	help available significant others concerned & willing to help	family & friends available but unwilling to help consistently, especially financially	mate, lover, family, therapist, clergy, employer hostile, exhausted or injurious to caller -or none
-communication	frequent positive interaction w/ more than one significant other	positive interaction with one significant other	little interaction with significant other(s)
-previous mental health contact	positive view of contact, ongoing relationship w/ therapist. or no experience but positive view	ambivalent or self-terminated relationship	negative view of help received; or no contact but negative view
5. Miscellaneous			
-history of suicide in family	none or distant relative	one close relative long time ago	one or more close relatives in recent past
-medical status	no significant medical problems	acute illness, psychosomatic illness (asthma, ulcers muscle cramps, hyperventilation)	chronic, debilitating or acute catastrophic illness
-life style history	fairly consistent work history, stable relationships, stable personality, no history of violent behavior	a crisis in a stable personality, perhaps a recent increase in longstanding disabling personality traits, some violence noted in past behavior, alcoholism or drug use	chronic suicidal behavior in unstable personality, recurrent outbreak of severe symptoms, difficulty in both family & job relationships, repeated violent outbursts, excessive substance abuse

Other impressions _____

_____

_____

_____

_____

				UNABLE TO
YOUR ASSESSMENT	_____LOW	_____MODERATE	_____HIGH	_____DETERMINE

HOMICIDE ASSESSMENT SHEET

PHONE: Name & No._____Date_____CALLER:_____

Name of potential perpetrator_____

Name of intended victim_____

I. First, complete the work sheet on the reverse side for probability of attempt variables. Using the completed worksheet, your experience, and your judgement, assess probability of attempt below (please circle)

PROBABILITY OF ATTEMPT: LOW   MEDIUM   HIGH

II. Describe Present Plan (include homicidal statements and clues)

III. Previous Homicide Attempts:
DATES: METHOD: OUTCOME:

_____
_____
_____

VI. Violence (ideation, behavior, impulse control)
DATES: METHOD: OUTCOME:

_____
_____
_____
_____

V. Significant Others (relatives, friends, therapists, helping agencies);
Name: Relationship: Address: Phone No. Present Communication

_____
_____
_____

VI. Ambivalence: Did the caller acknowledge ambivalence?_____
Non-homicidal Clues   Homicidal Clues

VIII. Plan of Action:
                    Own Resources: Outreach team:
_____No-homicide Decision   _____Consulted
_____Dispose of means   _____Implemented
_____Eat, Sleep, etc.   Emergency Procedure:
_____Recontact THE PHONE   _____Ambulance/Police sent
                External Resources:
_____Counseling
_____Contact Significant Other _____Warn Intended Victim
_____Follow-Up Call

****
DUTY TO WARN came from a court decision (Tarasoff, 1976) which stated that once a therapist makes an assessment of homicide that is "serious" (Medium-high probability) and the perpetrator is not hospitalized, the potential victim must be informed of the threat made on their life. The decision to warn the intended victim is important and needs to be made ONLY IN CONSULTATION WITH YOUR BACK-UP. It involves issues of assessment, confidentiality, working with the potential victim, and procedures for appropriate follow up.
****

Programs for People in Crisis

PROBABILITY OF ATTEMPT	LOW	MEDIUM	HIGH
1. HOMICIDE PLAN (describe on reverse) Details	__vague, no plan	__some specifics	__very specific, knows how, when, where
Time	__no specific time; in the future	__within a few hours	__Immediately, or in progress
Availability of means	__not available, will have to get	__available, have close by	__have in hand or in progress
Chance of intervention	__others present	__others available or expected	__no one nearby, isolated
2. PREVIOUS HOMICIDE ATTEMPTS	__none	__has exhibited aggressive behavior, been in fights but no attempts to kill anyone	__yes, looks at killing of another as a feasible act
3. PREVIOUS ARRESTS	__none	__has been arrested, has not served time	__multiple arrest history several times in prison
4. INTERNAL RESOURCES Anxiety	__Mild, some discomfort is felt	__moderate, discomfort is increasing but not overwhelming	__high, feels overwhelmed, may panic
Depression	__mild, feels slightly down	__occasional depression	__severe, chronically moody
Impulse Control	__controlled	__some impulsive acting out, not physically violent	__aggressive, feels need for violence
Hostility	__low	__some	__aggressive
Self Esteem	__good, has reinforcements from others	__usually good has times of being put down & not being able to handle it	__chronically poor self image
Isolation/Withdrawn	__able to relate well to other outgoing	__mild, some withdrawal and feelings of hopelessness	__long history of being a loner antisocial, withdrawn, hopeless, helpless
Drug/Alcohol Use	__nondrinker, occasional social drinker	__social drinker occasional abuse	__chronic abuse
Coping Strategies	__able to cope with stress and irritation	__usually can cope, some constricted thinking & acting out	__becomes constricted under stress, acts out in destructive socially unacceptable ways
Daily Functioning	__daily activities continue as usual with little change	__some daily activities are set aside, some disturbances in eating, sleeping & work habits	__many activities are discontinued gross disturbance in eating sleeping & work habits
Disorientation/ Disorganization	__is in good contact with what is happening	__little to moderate	__marked, losing contact with reality
5. EXTERNAL RESOURCES (as perceived by caller) Significant Others	__several reliable family/friends available	__few or one available	__none available
Resources	__able to use available resources	__some use, aware of some resources	__either unable to use or recognize available resources
6. LIFE STYLE HISTORY	__stable	__moderately stable	__unstable

*HAS is adapted from SAS-Baton Rouge Crisis Intervention Center and HOMICIDE by Nancy Allen.
B.R.C.I.C. - 7/85

RECALL SHEET

PHONE Name & No._____   Caller's Name_____

Date_____   Time:_____Began____Term. AM PM
    M   T   W   T   F   S   S
Line: 00   10   81   Total Time:_____Hours____Mins.

ADDITIONAL INFO: Log Book Page No._____
                                 Zip Code_____

I. What happened since last call?

II. Brief summary of this call. (Feeling and content)

III. Focus

IV. Affect and Behavior of caller during the call (Be specific)

V. Suicidal Assessment; See Pink Sheet:

VI. Did the caller follow through on referral and Previous Plan of Action?
    YES   NO   Explain (Be Specific)

VII. How did the conversation end? Plan of Action.

VIII. COUNSELOR'S Impressions and Feelings:

Was Back-Up consulted?_____Yes_____No
Was a Follow-Up arranged? ____Yes ____No
 -Purpose of FU/points to cover_____

Outcalls made in connection with this call____

IX. Staff Feedback:

FOLLOW UP CALL

PHONE Name & No._____

Date_____
  M   T   W   T   F   Sa   S

Additional Info:

Caller's Name_____ _____

Caller's Phone #_____ __

Time:_____Began_____Term   am   pɪ,

Total Time_____hours_____mins.

Log Book Page No._____

  I. Did Caller Follow Through on POA?

 II. What Happened Since Last Call?

III. Brief Summary of This Call (Feelings and Content)

 IV. Focus

  V. Affect and Behavior of Caller (Be Specific)

 VI. Suicidal Assessment, See Pink Sheet:

VII. How Did This Conversation End - Plan of Action.

VIII. COUNSELOR'S Impressions and Feelings.

IX. STAFF FEEDBACK:

CONSISTENT CALLER

PHONE Name and No. _____   Caller's Name _____

Date _____   Name used this call _____

M   T   W   Th   F   Sa   Su

Time _____Began_____Term   AM   PM

Line   00   10   81   :   8.

Total Time_____hours_____mins.

Additional Information:

Log Book Page No._____
Zip Code_____

Suicidal Assessment, See Pink Sheet:

I. Did caller follow through with Plan of Action on last call sheet?
What happened since the last call?

II. Brief Summary of this call. (Feelings and Content)

III. Focus.

IV. Affect and Behavior of caller during the call. (Be specific)

V.   How was this call terminated? What was the Plan of Action?

VI. COUNSELOR'S Impressions and Feelings.
     How does this call tie in with the Action Plan?

Was Back-Up consulted?_____Yes_____No

Was a Follow-Up call arranged?____Yes____No

-Purpose of FU/points to cover_____

Outcalls made in connection with this call_____

VII. STAFF FEEDBACK

BATON ROUGE CRISIS INTERVENTION CENTER, INC.-THE PHONE-5/82

GATEKEEPER PROGRAM
LIAISON CONTACT REPORT: BAR/LOUNGE

NAME OF ESTABLISHMENT_____

ADDRESS_____

TELEPHONE_____

MANAGER/OWNER_____

PERSON CONTACTED_____

POSITION_____

ALTERNATE CONTACT_____

POSITION_____

Initial Contact_____
Follow-up Contact_____
Telephone Contact_____

DATE:___/___/___ TIME:____A/PM

```
┌─────────────────────────────────────┐
│INITIAL CONTACT & CHANGES ONLY        │
│1. ____Neighborhood Bar (with         │
│        regular clientele)            │
│2. ____Hotel/Motel Bar                │
│3. ____Nightclub                      │
│4. ____Gay Bar                        │
│5. ____Singles Bar                    │
│6.  Capacity: _____               │
└─────────────────────────────────────┘
```

SUMMARY OF CONTACT (Use Reverse Side if Necessary):

MATERIALS PROVIDED: MATCHES _____ NAPKINS _____ OTHER _____

_____

ADDITIONAL REQUESTS: _____

SUGGESTIONS OF OTHER POTENTIAL GATEKEEPERS: _____

WAS GENERAL AGREEMENT FOR FUTURE CONTACT MADE: YES_____ NO_____WHEN:_____

GATEKEEPER LIAISON TEAM: _____/_____

HOURS EXPENDED BY EACH: _____/_____

BATON ROUGE CRISIS INTERVENTION CENTER, INC.
242 S_____

Action Plan for Consistent Caller

Completed by:_____   Caller:_____

Date completed:_____   Aliases:_____

Calling frequency:_____   Address:_____

Date of first call:_____   Phone:_____

Counseling Agency:_____   Sex:_____ Age:_____ Race:_____

Therapist:_____   S/M/D/W Living Situation:_____

Medication:_____   _____

Education/Occupation_____

Behavioral Type (see description under this sheet)_____

Significant Others (include names, phone #s, relationship quality):_____

_____

_____

_____

Affect & Behavioral Characteristics:_____

_____

_____

_____

_____

Usual Content:_____

_____

_____

_____

Suicidal Behavior:_____

_____

_____

Action Plan:_____

_____

_____

_____

_____

Appendix G: Program Evaluation Samples

AAS Certification Standards: Areas and Components

The AAS certification process includes evaluation of a crisis program in seven areas, with several components in each area (Wells and Hoff, 1984):

- Administration

    1. Governing body
    2. Program management
    3. Accountability: administration, personnel, and financial
    4. Physical setting

- Training program

    1. Planned curriculum objectives
    2. Planned curriculum content and bibliography
    3. Planned curriculum methodology
    4. Screening
    5. Pre- and post-evaluation of trainees
    6. Qualifications of trainers
    7. In-service training

- General service delivery system

    1. Telephone service
    2. Walk-in crisis service
    3. Outreach crisis service

    4. Follow up of crisis cases

    5. Client record-keeping

- Services in life-threatening crises

    1. Assessment of lethality

    2. Rescue capability

    3. Follow-up of persons attempting and threatening suicide or assault

    4. Suicide survivors services

    5. Follow-up of victims of violence

    6. Community education

- Ethical issues

    1. A code of ethics

    2. Security of records

    3. Confidentiality

    4. Ethical rescue procedures

    5. Advertising and promotional methods

- Community integration

    1. Consumers

    2. Emergency resources

    3. Resource data

    4. Mental-medical health and social service agencies

    5. General community resources

- Program evaluation

    1. Program objectives

    2. Evaluation—content

    3. Evaluation—extent

    4. Implementation

    5. Utilization of evaluation outcomes

Programs seeking certification are evaluated by examination of written materials describing the agency's operation and through a site visit by two Regional Certification Committee members. Data from agency documents, interviews, and observation are used as the basis for evaluation. The evaluation team rates the program on a score sheet (see Score Sheet on p. 193) according to predefined standards ranging from Level I to Level IV, the highest standard. The evaluation procedures include qualitative and quantitative methods and are adapted from the work of W. Wolfensberger's Program Evaluation of Service Systems (PAAS).

AAS Certificate Report ▬▬▬▬▬▬▬▬▬▬▬▬▬

SCORE SHEET

Crisis Program _____ Director _____

Address _____ Telephone ( ) _____

City _____ State _____ Zip _____

Previous AAS Evaluations(s) _____ Date(s) _____

Currently AAS Certified: Yes___ No___

INSTRUCTIONS: Place an X in the column under the level which best describes the program.

SCORING: Level I = 0, Level II = 1, Level III = 2, Level IV = 3.
The number in parentheses under each area total is the minimum allowable score for initial certification. Any score falling in a shaded area precludes certification.

LEVEL RATING

AREA	COMPONENT	I	II	III	IV	
I: ADMINISTRATION	1. Governing Body	■				Area I Score
	2. Program Management					
	3. Accountability					
	4. Physical Setting					(6)
II: TRAINING PROCEDURES	1. Planned Curriculum Objectives	■				Area II Score
	2. Curriculum Content. Bibliography	■				
	3. Planned Methodology					
	4. Screening	■				(11)
	5. Pre-, Post-Training Evaluation					
	6. Qualification of Trainers	■				
	7. Inservice Training					
III: GENERAL SERVICE DELIVERY SYSTEM	1. Telephone Service	■				Area III Score
	2. Walk-In Service					
	3. Outreach Service					
	4. Follow-Up of Crisis Cases					(8)
	5. Client Recordkeeping					
IV: SERVICES IN LIFE-THREATENING CRISES	1. Assessment of Lethality	■				Area IV Score
	2. Rescue Capability					
	3. Follow-Up: Attempter,Threatener					
	4. Survivor Services					(9)
	5. Follow-Up of Victims					
	6. Community Education					
V: ETHICAL ISSUES	1. Code of Ethics	■				Area V Score
	2. Security of Records					
	3. Confidentiality					
	4. Rescue Procedures					(8)
	5. Advertising, Promotions					
VI: COMMUNITY INTEGRATION	1. Consumers	■				Area VI Score
	2. Emergency Rescue Resources					
	3. Resource Data					
	4. Health & Social Services	■				(8)
	5. General Resources					
VII: PROGRAM EVALUATION	1. Objectives	■				Area VII Score
	2. Evaluation-Content					
	3. Evaluation-Extent					
	4. Implementation	■				(7)
	5. Utilization of Outcomes					

TOTAL SCORE _____

Signature of Examiners: Date:

_____   _____

_____   _____

SITE VISIT EVALUATION FORM

Directions: This form is to be completed by the center director (or designee) and returned to the Chief Certification Examiner.

Note: This evaluation will not affect the certification outcome.

RATING SCALE: 1 - very satisfactory
2 - satisfactory
3 - very unsatisfactory

1. Arrangements for the site visit:

1	2	3	4	5
very satisfactory		satisfactory		very satisfactory

Comments:

2. Thoroughness of the site visit:

1	2	3	4	5
very satisfactory		satisfactory		very satisfactory

Comments:

3. Attitude of examiners:

1	2	3	4	5
very satisfactory		satisfactory		very satisfactory

Comments:

4. Helpfulness of examiners: (including final report, if available when this form is completed)

1	2	3	4	5
very satisfactory		satisfactory		very satisfactory

Comments:

5. Objectivity of examiners:

1	2	3	4	5
very satisfactory		satisfactory		very satisfactory

Comments:

6. What did you like best about the site visit?

7. What did you dislike about the site visit?

8. Suggestions for improvement:

9. Name of Program_____ Date of Site Visit_____

AMERICAN ASSOCIATION OF SUICIDOLOGY

EVALUATION REPORT - RECERTIFICATION

AAS Certification Committee - Region II

Name of Agency: Greater County Crisis Service, Inc.

Address: 1985 East-West Avenue
                     Middletown, Alaska 12345

Telephone: (603) 736-1960

Agency Director: Miriam Crisis

Date of Site Evaluation: February 27, 1985

Certification Examiners: Marianne Konsolt, Ph.D.
                            Edward Evaluator, M.S.W.

INTRODUCTION:

The Crisis Service is a program of the Mental Health Association of
greater Middletown, a United Way agency. Although previously
certified by the AAS, the certification had lapsed for several years.
This evaluation is based upon material submitted prior to and during
the site visit, inspection of the facility, and interviews with the
following people:

Charles Batchelder	Executive Director, MHA
Miriam Crisis	Director, GCCS
Ruth Inservice	Training Specialist, GCCS
Mildred Wagner	Board Member, MHA
Penny Downing	Outreach Coordinator, Middletown MHC
Jordan Cornog	Volunteer
Richard Moore	Volunteer
China Lao	Volunteer

The site visit began at 8:30 a.m. and ended at 5:30 p.m., including a
luncheon meeting with two members of the Board, the Executive Director
of the Mental Health Association, the Program Director of Crisis Service,
and the Training Specialist.

GCCS operates out of four rooms in the Middletown Community Hospital
complex. It serves the area of Greater County, Alaska, a 424 square
mile area located in the Juneau area. A significant number of its
100,000 residents are State employees, military personnel, or providers
of support services for the government. The organization was originally
incorporated in February of 1975 as Crisis, Inc., but in November of last
year it changed its name to Greater County Crisis Service, Inc.

One of the most remarkable aspects of this recertification process was
the active participation of the Board of Directors in preparing for the

site visit. This involvement, along with the center's charismatic and efficient
Director, Miriam Crisis, is reflected in the way the center's Board and staff are
able to unite and direct their activities to the changing moods of the community.

EVALUATION

AREA I: Administration

The agency attained a score of 10 in this area, out of a possible 12. The governing
body has, within the last two years, moved this from an all counselor Board to
include 5 community members and 10 volunteers. We applaud this direction as a
way to avoid the myopia that can result from a policy-making body that is totally
immersed in the day-to-day operation of the program. Also, the Agency's funding
base, which is currently heavily depedent on foundation grants, might be
strengthened by judicious selection of community Board members. At present, GCCS
can assure approximately 60% of its funding from year to year.

The table of organization shows an inconsistency in that the scheduler should be
placed under the supervision of the Coordinator of Volunteer Services.

The Agency's cost per unit of service is very reasonable: $2.75, because of the
extensive and judicious use of volunteers. The Agency is in the process of locating
expanded facilities; however, we think that the staff and volunteers have managed
very effectively in somewhat congested space.

> Recommendations:
>
> 1. Consider adding more community members to the Board of Directors to
>   strengthen its position in the community and increase local support.
> 2. Continue the effort to develop contracts with other agencies for
>   coverage provided; seek public and other funding resources which
>   provide a more stable base. At present, a very substantial amount of
>   the Director's time is spent in fundraising; and while she is
>   apparently very successful, her talents and administrative abilities
>   are needed in other areas of Agency operation as well.

AREA II: Training Procedures

The Agency, after completing a bibliography, received a score of 12 in this area,
out of a possible 21. As in other areas, program objectives need to be stated
in measurable terms. The training methodology is newly organized; the hours of
training considerably exceed the recommended minimum. Screening is done in
groups of up to seven people.

The training program utilizes the experiences and talents of GCCS volunteers in
a very effective way and brings in people from the community to provide information
in particular areas.

The Agency is to be commended for developing a continuing education committee
comprised of volunteers. They plan the monthly in-service training meetings;
volunteers are required to attend ten hours of in-service, one of which is a
mandatory, yearly suicide prevention refresher course.

Supervision is problematic. Experienced Senior Workers are given a great deal of
responsibility in the Agency, and there is a newly implemented annual conference
held with each volunteer for evaluation purposes. Nevertheless, supervision
does not occur on a formalized, regular basis, but is rather viewed more as

consultation when needed or troubleshooting when problems are picked up by the Senior Worker or staff member.

Recommendations:

1. Refine further the training objectives in behaviorally stated terms.
2. Conduct individual screening interviews with applicants; these should be conducted by two people who are specially trained in interviewing strategies.
3. Provide each guest instructor who participates in training with a clear syllabus and recommended methodology to assure complete relevance to the Agency's training objectives.
4. Compile the resource materials which are now handed out at each session into a training manual which is indexed for easy accessibility and reference.
5. Use the Cluster Groups for group supervision. These could meet monthly and provide an opportunity for supervision and support. The structure is already in place; it needs only to be redefined and implemented as an effective mechanism. Staff members could float, and thus add to the quality of supervision.

AREA III: General Service Delivery System

In this area, the Center achieved a score of 14, only one less than the maximum score of 15.

Since the last site visit, three years ago, the Center has made great progress in reducing the number of repeat callers. This success may be related, in part, to implementation of the 1984 site visitor's suggestion to discourage caller anonymity.

Outreach visits still average only 10 per year in the 100,000 population area served. This low average suggests an area for evaluation regarding real community needs for outreach and determination of whether or note police are handling these crises by default. Outreach staff might consider developing a police ride-along plan as a means of gaining some "inside" knowledge about the low outreach rate and possible need to expand this program.

Records are sometimes incomplete and support other observations about the sporadic nature of the supervisory process. For example, appropriate feedback was missing on an incomplete call, while staff doing record monitoring followed up on a questionable lethality assessment by a volunteer.

Recommendation:

1. The extent and overall excellence of the general service delivery system may be further enhanced by the Center's careful collaboration in a program being planned by a local hospital regarding the management of behavioral emergencies.

AREA IV: Services in Life-Threatening Crises

The rating in this area is 10 out of a possible 18, one point above the minimum requirement of nine.

The Suicide Survivor Service is well planned and well implemented. The Crisis Service sponsors a group for survivors called Coping with Suicide which meets twice a month and is facilitated by a staff member and a volunteer. Referrals

to the group come mainly from newpaper announcements and the Crisis Service.
Services for victims of crime are less well developed.

The community education component of the Crisis Service seems to come largely
from the Mental Health Association. Flyers, bookmarks, tent cards are used
effectively. A Gatekeepers program is in the planning stage.

Recommendations:

1.   Revise follow-up policies. As follow-up calls are not routine and
     instigated primarily from volunteers' assessments, closer scrutiny
     of call sheets and volunteer assessment sills is needed.
2.   Expand referrals to the Survivors' group by contacting local funeral
     directors and coroner.
3.   Keep more thorough records on the members of the Survivors' group.
4.   Continue the new policy of initiating contact with people who may be in
     crisis (the third party).

AREA V: Ethical Issues

The Agency scored 14 out of a possible 15 points in this area.

GCCS has developed a Code of Ethics based on several models and integrated into the
Agency's own practice needs. They have consulted with lawyers on such issues as
tracing and breaking and entering. Record security is well maintained, and volunteers
are carefully trained in confidentiality issues. No client information is stored
or kept in the rooms in which clients are seen or areas used by clients. Records are
kept locked, and all staff interviewed, including the secretary, gave responses
consistent with policy on issues relating to records and confidentiality. Advertising
materials are tasteful and appropriate, and many have been developed by professionals
in the fields.

AREA VI: Community Integration

The Agency received nine out of a possible 15 points in this area.

Because there is no formalized publicity program, there is limited effort to
identify and reach specific target groups, for example, victims of crime. The
Agency responds, when possible, to requests for presentations, but does so
primarily through the staff and a few volunteers.

The Agency's resource material is extremely well-organized, thanks to the
careful services of a volunteer who keeps the material updated and clearly
accessible to counselors.

Recommendations:

1.   Consider the development of a Speakers' Bureau which might be comprised
     of experienced volunteers as well as staff.
2.   Proceed with plans to upgrage the public relations aspect of the
     program.
3.   Include in the above effort a plan to indentify target groups who
     are not utilizing the Agency's services (e.g. adolescents, elderly,
     victims of crime, etc.) and provide specifically focused community
     education programming for these groups.
4.   In addition to the blue page advertising in the telephone directory,
     consider listings in the white and yellow pages under Suicide and

Crisis Services.

AREA VII: Program Evaluation

In this area, a score of 10 was achieved out of a possible 15.

In spite of the long standing excellence of this Agency's program, the staff do not seem to "rest on their laurels" but rather keep alert to ways of improving service. The climate of research and evaluation that charaterizes the GCCS is revealed in the fact that two doctoral disserations and five master's theses have been produced through student affiliations with the Center. Evaluation of suicide attempters in emergency rooms revealed 100% follow-through. The Board of Self Evaluation Committee made detailed suggestions regarding program evaluation which are thoroughly supported by the certification examiners.

Recommendations:

1. Program objectives could be written in more measurable terms, e.g. change, "Increase the number of calls from youth" to Increase the number of calls from those under 20 from X% to Y% by the end of the fiscal year."
2. In fifteen caller records reviewed, the question about where they live has been asked in only one. Consider utilizing the space for a "question of the month" - or week, etc. Prominently post the question and expect listeners will ask it.

SUMMARY AND RECOMMENDATION

Greater County Crisis Service, Inc. is operating above the minimum standards established by the American Association of Suicidology. It is our pleasure to recommend certification.

Marianne Konsolt, Ph.D.
Certification Coordinator, Region II

Edward Evaluator, M.S.W.
Certification Examiner

INDEX